MW00338879

Silentium

And Other Reflections On Memory, Sorrow, Place, and the Sacred

Connie T. Braun

Foreword by Jean Janzen

RESOURCE *Publications* · Eugene, Oregon

SILENTIUM
And Other Reflections On Memory, Sorrow, Place, and the Sacred

Resource Publications
An Imprint of Wipf and Stock Publishers
199 W. 8th Ave., Suite 3
Eugene, OR 97401

www.wipfandstock.com

PAPERBACK ISBN: 978-1-5326-1792-8
HARDCOVER ISBN: 978-1-4982-4302-5
EBOOK ISBN: 978-1-4982-4301-8

Manufactured in the U.S.A.   09/25/17

with love
to the one who shares my story

because of
our children and grandchildren

dedicated to
those who were children then

in memory of
Wilhelm and Jakobine

There are so many things you would never think to tell anyone. And I believe they may be the things that mean most to you, and that even your own child would have to know in order to know you well at all.

—Rev. John Ames
Gilead by Marilyn Robinson, 102

I have come to see that the past is always changing, never static, never "placed" forever like a book on a shelf. As we grow and change, we understand things and the people who have influenced us in new ways.

—May Sarton
A House by the Sea, 95

Contents

Quiet

Repose

Foreword

With her lyrical sense of life and history, Connie T. Braun offers her readers a poignant narrative of both tragedy and resilience. Giving voice to the history of her mother's family in Poland during and after World War II, she records her personal search of a haunting and bare survival. The story of Mennonites in Poland, which has been essentially untold for decades, waits for a faithful telling, the courage to enter unknown territory and to listen to what lies hidden. This collection of essays and poems is the fruit of this author's faith in the human spirit and story as she breaks the silence, testifying to unfinished histories.

Braun takes us with her into the actual landscape of her mother's memories, which becomes a journey of a geography of the self, a movement into her mother's memories with a search for meanings. Traveling with her, we enter the power of place and untold memory of profound losses and senseless violence witnessed by a child. As she seeks for language, the metaphor of knitting and crocheting becomes an emblem of the search for pattern in a story that could have easily slipped off the needle, but might also be salvaged by a stitch at the right time. "Grief is a long migration," she writes, taking us with her on this journey, that loose yarn leading at last to an open border and, finally, safety. Her description of the family's escape into Germany and a refugee camp, and then, at last, permission to enter Canada, becomes the story of her own existence.

"We are born into an elegy," this author reminds us, the grief of dispossession and displacement continuing into this century. It is important to listen to the witness, and in that act we become a witness. This book invites the reader to enter into this power of memory and place, to allow its darkness to be transformed into the possibility of recovery and even beauty, because "the silent bell must be rung."

Jean Janzen
Fresno, California

Acknowledgments

The following essays were first presented at various literary conferences:

"Pilgrimage" *Mennonite/s Writing VIII: Personal Narratives of Place and Displacement*, University of Winnipeg, Winnipeg, Manitoba, 2017.

"Oral History" *Crossing the Line: Women of Anabaptist Traditions Encounter Borders and Boundaries*, Eastern Mennonite University, Virginia, 2017.

"Between Worlds (or Poland 1973)" *Global Mennonite Peace Conference*, Conrad Grebel University, Waterloo, Ontario, 2016.

"Crochet: or a Story of the Immigrant Family" *Mennonite/s Writing VII: Movement, Transformation, Place,* Fresno Pacific University, California, 2015. Published in *The Journal for the Center of Mennonite Writing*, Goshen, 2017.

"Nothing but Words" was presented as "An Inheritance of Words— Poetry at the Crossing of Borders" at the *Western Literature Association*, Victoria, British Columbia, 2014.

"A Walk in the Old Country" was presented as "A Return to Old Country: Travelling the Landscape of Chaos through Silence, Memory and Imagination" at the *Verge SAMC Arts and Narrative Conference*, Trinity Western University, Langley, British Columbia, September 2013.

"Silence, Memories, and Elegies: An Inheritance of Words Unspoken" *Mennonite/s Writing Conference VI: Solos and Harmonies*, Eastern Mennonite University, Virginia, 2011.

Poems in this collection of meditative, lyric, memoir, biographical, and personal essays have been published in *The Journal of Mennonite Writing* (Goshen College, Indiana) 2012, and in *Mennonite Mothering*, Demeter Press (Bradford, Ontario) 2013, and collected in *UnSpoken: An Inheritance of Words*, Fern Hill Publications, Vancouver, 2016.

Acknowledgments

Where I have relied on family documents, newspaper articles, unpublished memoirs and works by various writers, or quoted writers, I have made references to them in my writing. These include: the newspaper article, "In die Heimat: und doch nicht noch Hause," *Mennonitische Rundschau*, September 1973, pg. 12, written by my grandfather Wilhelm D. Schroeder, along with his personal notes, *Aufzeichnungen von Wilhelm D. Schroeder über sein Leben, im Jahre* 1965, translated by Ella (Schroeder) Strumpski; the self-published memoir by Colin P. Neufeldt, *Unsere Familie: A Pictorial History of the Ratzlaff, Janzen, Pauls and Schmidt Families* (2006) that offers a few details of the evacuation and refugee flight of 1945; and newspaper articles by Robert Foth, "Geschichte der Mennoniten und MB Gemeinden zu Deutsch Wymschle, Polen. Die Verfolgung der Deutschen in Polen (1938–1939)" published in *Mennontische Rundschau*, June 5th and July 3rd, 1968; along with Eric L. Ratzlaff's self-published memoir (1983) *From the Fraser to the Don: Research and Reminiscence—a Personal Family History of Eric Leonard Ratzlaff*. In 1982, Wojciech Marchlewski, a university student at the University of Warsaw, working on a master's thesis about the Dutch Settlements of Mazovia (in Poland), wrote to Eric L. Ratzlaff for information on the Mennonites. Much of his scholarship pertaining to the early settlements relies on Ratzlaff's own research and writing. Mr. Marchlewski subsequently conducted post-doctoral studies on the Mennonites of the Mazovia region north of Warsaw that includes Wymyschle and Kazun, and casts further light on the experience of my mother's family in Poland during and after 1945.

I have made every effort to offer material that is consistent from source to source and to note where there are any discrepancies.

With respect to names of cities and towns, I have indicated how they are used in the context of history. Otherwise I retain the German spelling of the village Wymyschle as my family knew it. The spelling of "Mennonite" foods ranges widely from German to Low-German. I use the spelling given in the *Mennonite Treasury of Recipes* and in *Mennonite Foods and Folkways from South Russia*. There are some adaptations of Polish words to the Low-German dialect; for example, *Babcia* (grandmother) is *Babtjche*.

Acknowledgments

Special thanks and love to my mother, Erna (Schroeder) Letkeman for sharing her memories, but more so, this book is written with my deepest gratitude for her quiet inspiration.

Thanks also to aunts Ella (Schroeder) Strumpski and Anna (Schroeder) Ratzlaff, and uncles John Schroeder and Henry Schroeder for providing information via interviews, family photographs, primary documents, and personal unpublished memoirs pertaining to the family's past life in Poland.

As a writer, my gratitude goes to Wayne Grady for his support and his comments on the very first drafts of these essays, and to Lynn Szabo, Marlene Epp, Dorothy Peters, and Tanya Bellehumeur Allat for their valuable insights as I polished them into this book. My deep appreciation goes to Ann Hostetler, and to the *Mennonite/s Writing* circle of writers and scholars, who have created space for the poems and stories I offer. To Jean Janzen, who has walked this path ahead of me: I am honored that you open this book with a foreword.

To my friend Birgit who knew about this project before I wrote the first sentence: your vision and words of encouragement have been my inspiration.

To Sharon: childhood, Europe as teenagers, and lifelong friendship, this is our shared journey, but you have traveled through the Valley of Shadows. Sarah's little light shines.

Alecia, my daughter and initial copy editor, thanks for highlighting my imperfections! Seriously, your response to my work means the world to me, and although you say my stories make you cry, yours bring me laughter, and you give me joy.

Finally, my thanks go to Brian Palmer, Ian Creeger, Matthew Wimer, and Wipf and Stock for transforming my manuscript into this book.

Introduction

It is the season of Lent once again, as I attend (on Ash Wednesday, 2017) to the final touches of this manuscript before publication. This year, in my readings for Lent, the poet priest Malcolm Guite writes that Lent is a time of going upstream to the source.[1] How apt his words, in life, and in writing this book wherein I have gone upstream to the source. Not only to the beginnings of my ancestral faith tradition. And not only from the present to the past. But also from Gdansk, Poland, upstream to the village of Wymyschle.

The American memoirist Patricia Hampl has said that life had given her the themes of her Catholic faith and her American-Czech heritage.[2] Life has given me the strands of my heritage which intertwines German ancestry and Mennonite Anabaptist belief. As a Canadian writer of witness (non-fiction and poetry), dispossession is a topic I often address, given to me by birth. As a child of immigrants who experienced dispossession and displacement as refugees of World War II, I write as one ascertaining and trying to understand my place in time and in the world. I think also of the present day when the number of refugees and those displaced rivals that war. And of how, within these stories, not only words, but silences also speak meaning.

Located at the heart, and middle, of this book, are painful stories. They are the "long Saturday" as George Steiner has described those three days central to Christian history.[3] Such inchoate stories of violent histories—surviving first in obscurity and passing through the various stages of silence that are effected by trauma—wish to be given a voice. After the

---

1. Guite, *The Word in the Wilderness*, 6.

2. Hampl, *Tell Me True*, 141.

3. *Steiner, Real Presences*, 232.

passing of time, and after mourning, in quietude and repose, the stories can be told. This is evidence of the power and mystery of the human spirit. I have observed that from the ground of loss flourished my grandmother's uncomplicatedness, contentment, unconditional love, and faith. She seemed to accept that, at the deepest level, dispossession is the human condition. From birth we are dispossessed of our first and primal place of refuge. All of life thereafter moves us toward our final dispossession, although her—my—heritage teaches that death is penultimate, is not the last word.

At the heart of my stories of loss is the leitmotif of regeneration. I write attesting to the remarkableness of the human spirit, with its propensity for love, joy, compassion, to be known, and to the silent groaning for life's fullness that finds its voice as story. These essays may be read in the order they are presented, or as the reader pleases, but together, or individually, I trust they convey the veracity of story as life-giving. To be truthful about what is painful is how we heal. And as the writer Eva Hoffman states, "mourning is at the root of all knowledge."[4] Our stories add to the fullness of history, and as the philosopher Paul Ricoeur posited, history belongs to us all.[5] Stories of the past give us a way forward, a future.

4. Hoffman, *After Such Knowledge*, 190.
5. Kearney, *States of Mind*, 228.

1

Silentium
(out of the silence)

The silkworms on the leaves, the pupae inside the yellow cloudlike whorl of filaments. From this, thread is spun by a woman working wordlessly at the wheel, the thread dyed bright colors before being placed on the loom and the weaver fashions the strands into cloth. It is a long and quiet process.

〜

How would I describe silence? Do I listen to it?

The other day as I walked home in the rain along busy Burrard Street, I saw a sign in the door of a century-old church that said, "Sanctuary Open." As I walked by, my mind was preoccupied with my husband's upcoming open-heart surgery and our daughter's overdue baby, but an impulse overtook me and I turned around. I walked up the steps to the entrance of the stone church and pulled open the wooden doors. Inside, the empty church was a silent space bathed in soft light streaming in through stained glass. I took a seat in a pew near the back.

A well-known author, Kathleen Norris, describes how she was asked to visit a classroom and played a game with the young students that first involved making noise, then being still. When she asked small children to describe noise, she was not surprised that the descriptions were clichés (like a herd of elephants). Conversely, when she asked the children to describe silence, the children responded with descriptions such as "silence is like a spider spinning a web" or "a silkworm making silk."[1] This author observed that only when the children were in a calm and peaceful environment were they able to listen to what she was asking them to do and able to reach a point of stillness. She was also making a point about the silence of the beautiful and mysterious that children seemed naturally open to.

Remember catching snowflakes on the tongue? The soundlessness of a gentle winter snowfall? How the slate sky, pregnant with moisture, held the promise of beauty and the anticipation of joy? Beyond this, what we couldn't see or know, every unseen ice nucleus within a water droplet forming a snowflake, until the *sky was filled* and heavy, they floated to earth.

One of the children in the class described silence in this way, "silence is me sleeping, waiting to wake up."[2] I know the child quoted was referring to that first state of being, a refuge of peace.

When have I thought of waiting as peaceful? And yet, this is what spirituality would teach us.

Silence is an open space—capacious, calm—a sanctuary amid the din of life.

~

Just as water is expressed in a great variety of forms, silence is a multivalent presence within the human experience. *Silentium*: silence, meaning stillness, quiet, repose, and also obscurity. Every life, from the beginning, is an inchoate story to someday be told.

We've been expecting his/her arrival for over a week now, and still we wait, despite the early contractions promising birth. The due date has passed. This unborn child, in the waters within the mother's body, is obscured from our full knowledge of him or her. And the child is still obscured from the world where, it is certain, the child will know both the state of innocence, the stillness of it like a ripple-free lake in the early summer morning—and the loss of it.

Silentium also means a place of silence. Within the cocoon of a mother's womb, transformed from cells into a fully developed fetus, a child is waiting.

1. Norris, *Amazing Grace*, 17.
2. Ibid., 17.

His or her cells are part of the lives who came before, and will continue on in the lives that may come after, a continuum woven mysteriously from the strands of our DNA. Something of me is in my daughter, and something of her will remain in this child. But this child will, as we all do, live out his or her own particular story.

~

On the ultrasound image, before anything can be heard, the heart appears as a dot [.], small as a grain of pepper or a poppy seed. In obscurity it forms and pulses, even before the cells fashion a tadpole-like body, the nubs of limbs and eyes and mouth.

When my husband was unborn, his heart taking shape in obscurity, his aortic valve developed only two of its three flaps. As he grew, unaffected, this small defect remained unnoticed, until mid-life when, in a routine examination, the doctor placed a stethoscope to his chest and discerned the slightest murmur. Imaging showed the blood passing into and leaking out of his heart's chambers; abstract splashes of blue and red, interpreted to mean he would require open heart surgery to replace the valve.

Two days past her due date, I drove my daughter to the hospital for monitoring, the protocol when overdue to determine the stress on the baby. The young woman performing the scan could tell that the amniotic fluid was at the low end of normal. The ultrasound image showed the head down, posterior, the baby's back curved against the swell of its mother's stomach, each intricate vertebrae of the tiny perfect spine like a string of beads. Then an image of the umbilical cord vigorously pulsing blood from the mother to baby, vibrant flashes of blue and red! Everything seemed fine.

In another room to monitor the heartbeat during contractions, my daughter joined three other mothers lying on gurneys, bare bellies like foothills. Each of the mothers was hooked up to sound, and the room filled with the rhythm of hearts beating like hoofs; fillies and colts bounding over fields. Our baby's heart rate rose from 138 to 145 as my daughter's belly tightened.

It is now the day before our daughter's scheduled induction, and my husband and I are in the hematologist's office discussing heart valve options, blood viscosity and the possibility of blood clots, blood thinners—things we need to decide on before my husband's surgery can be scheduled, which could be any day now. The specialist checks his blood pressure. 142 over 80; good.

〜

When we fall in love, or have children, we enter a silent contract, one we haven't fully considered, but are willing to take the risk for the pure joy it also promises. But joy and sorrow are monozygotic—of the same origin—like paternal twins.

"I can't believe we will forget our sorrows altogether. That would mean forgetting that we had lived, humanly speaking. Sorrow seems to me to be a great part of the substance of human life," said the old Reverend John Ames in the novel *Gilead*, by Marilynne Robinson.[3] Misfortune, the burdens we bear, even grief, the Reverend is saying, allow us to understand what it really means to be human. We begin to understand this more the older we grow, but for the most part, it remains a mystery.

〜

Grief is a bifurcating force that cuts right through flesh and bone and heart.

In grief, silence is an absence. Silence is a presence.

〜

Sharon worked full-time and was looking forward to her maternity leave when she could be at home with the new baby and her three-year-old. The weather had been hot that whole week in July, and so her little daughter was especially excited about visiting relatives who had a backyard pool. It would be a special outing.

In hot weather, it takes only minutes, the fire department spokesperson stated in the article under the headline, "Three-year-old Drowns in Swimming Pool."

When I heard the news that day at the end of July 1992, I drove from my parents' lake house for hours with my own three small children to my Cousin Sharon's house, trying to get there, as if there were something I might be able to do. There were no words of comfort to offer her. I didn't know what to say. When I saw her, we embraced. I cried and told her only, "I don't know what to say."

---

3. Robinson, *Gilead*, 104.

Silence is sorrow's tongue.

Perhaps our aged grandmother had the only words tolerable; she, in her eighth decade at this time, Sarah's great-grandmother. "The little child won't know suffering," she had stated. Words to console? Or simply to offer a truth when life makes no sense? I only heard this second-hand, but it's true our grandmother had known sorrow, deep as Sharon's. She had not forgotten the unnaturalness of what it is like for a mother to survive her child, the aberration of such grief. She, who had lost a child in the first weeks of its infancy, and a teenage son to a senseless war, and who had started over in a new country when she was fifty. Loss always leads us into unknown territory.

The writer May Sarton, in her later years, writing about both the richness of relationships and bereavement, considered the idea in her journals[4] that sorrows *can* be absorbed and accepted, weaving themselves into a life, becoming part of its meaning. Perhaps it takes a long life before one can say this authentically, accepting it, knowing it as a truth.

Sarah's coffin was small and oyster white. I will never forget the sight of it as I looked back, bright in that summer afternoon among the grave stones and the green rolling lawn of the cemetery, and how, after all the mourners had taken their leave, the young parents remained by the gravesite.

Two months later, September 14th, Sharon gave birth to a son, Eric. Though the spelling was different, Sarah had picked the name for the new baby, if a brother, after playing with my five-year-old son, Erik. September 23rd would have been Sarah's birthday.

Not long after, I went out with Sharon, her newborn Eric in the stroller. A stranger stopped us to admire the baby. "Is this your first?" she asked. Looking at Sharon, I didn't speak. But she sought her own words, as if they were air. "No, my first child died just before he was born. Her name was Sarah. She was almost four."

⁓

It is our most basic instinct of all, to *live*.

⁓

4. See May Sarton, *House by the Sea*, and *Journal of Solitude*.

The poet Gregory Orr, as a child, experienced the traumatic death of his brother in a hunting accident. The title of one of his books is *Poetry as Survival*. In it, Orr describes how poetry and stories are the human impulse to make some sort of sense out of what we experience, and if not to seek an answer, then, at best, in some way to regain a semblance of order from confusion; in order to overcome the silence that arrives in the aftermath of chaos and threatens to remain; to move from the silence of oblivion, towards life.[5]

We remember so that we will live.

At times, over coffee, we discuss our grown children—my daughter and two sons, Sharon's son and two younger daughters. In between our words is silence pregnant with memory.

~

According to a Russian priest, "To say to anyone I love you is tantamount to saying you shall live forever," writes Madeleine L'Engle in her memoir.[6] In love lies a kind of resurrection.

Ruth, the young orphaned narrator in Marilynn Robinson's *Housekeeping*, a book about the impermanence of things, asks what our memories are for. Why do our thoughts recall the intimate gestures of a loved one? Why does our mind return us to the particular details of a specific afternoon? And why do memories come, like an unexpected visitor from long ago? "What are all these fragments for if not to be knit up finally?"[7]

As finite beings, with beginnings and endings, we have always been interested in storymaking as evidenced by the silent shapes of antelope dancing and fish swimming on cave walls. From earliest mythology, humankind has been preoccupied with story, its immortal beings and gods, from the Epic of Gilgamesh to the Biblical story of Genesis, each narrative is a quest to comprehend life's origins. From what fragments was the universe "knit up?" The universe is discovered to be continually expanding, but who can truly say when the universe began? Or how?

5. Orr, *Poetry as Survival*, 18.
6. L'Engle, *Circle of Quiet*, 110.
7. Robinson, *Housekeeping*, 92.

Telling a story has to do with faith—faith that the universe has meaning and that our human lives are not irrelevant.[8] This view is held by religion and philosophy alike; this compulsion for meaning in life is what makes us uniquely *human*. The "knitting up" of memory into storymaking is the human endeavor to assemble coherence from particles, to bestow meaning to our lives and another's—a sacred, god-like act.

"I remember when you were born, there was a spring storm outside. . . ." Often I have told the story of her birth to my daughter, now anticipating the birth of her own child knit up in her womb as the psalmist describes this process of creation. Her baby will be the first grandchild on both sides of family, the first great-grandchild. Out of the silence, a genealogy spun like a silk thread, and on the loom a new and particular story.

8. L 'Engle, *Circle of Quiet,* 194.

Obscurity

2

A Walk in the Old Country

In her poem, "Lake of Two Rivers" the Canadian poet Anne Michaels writes these lines: *My mother's story is tangled / overgrown with lives of parents and grandparents / because they lived in one house and among them / remembered hundreds of years of history.*[1] My mother's story also is tangled and overgrown with the lives of others in the house in Poland where she was born. Imperceptible intersections, strong as spider-thread, but just as fine.

⁓

My mother and all her siblings were born in the same house, twelve births in all. Peter, the second-born, lived only a few days. Their mother, my grandmother, had come to live in the house when she was an infant. It was the home of her foster parents, Heinrich and Paulina, because her own mother had died when she was three days old. My grandmother was named after her mother, Jacobine. When my grandmother married at twenty, she and my grandfather assumed the responsibility of the aging couple's farm, and three generations lived together under one roof.

That day, when my grandmother was in labor, it had been raining all afternoon. When the neighbor, the midwife, arrived, the oldest son, David, patient and responsible, led his two younger brothers, Heinrich (Henry), age twelve, and Johann (John), ten, out of the fray of six children cooped up inside in winter, and up to the attic where the boys occupied themselves with the roosting pigeons. Martha, eight, and Anna, six, were under the

1. Michaels, *The Weight of Oranges/Miner's Pond*, 7.

watchful eye of an aunt who came to help with the household chores, and they in turn would have amused little Wilhelm (later called Bill) and two-year-old Emilie. That afternoon, February 18th, 1939, my mother was born.

It was the year Hitler would invade Poland.

Dispossessed of house and home when she was a child, my mother's history was silent until long after I was grown and I sought to recover it. I am recollecting all of this following my first trip to Poland in August 2005.

~

I'm on a train towards memory. The landscape here seems familiar; the fields and hills, the low mountains that border the valley and the quilt of farms spread out between them. It reminds me of the Fraser Valley in British Columbia where I was born, and before that, where, after immigrating to Canada, my grandparents purchased a small ten-acre farm in the Sumas Prairie. After the war.

Their oldest child, David, was just seventeen when he was conscripted in Poland. He was killed one month before his nineteenth birthday. My grandparents arrived in Canada, in 1951, with ten surviving children. They demonstrated what being thankful looked like. What *enough* looked like. A pot of chicken noodle soup simmering, freshly baked buns, always enough for anyone who dropped in. My Grandmother wiping the plastic tablecloth to set the plates, and over the table, a verse inscribed on a plaque, "Give us this day our daily bread." After they sold the farm, they moved to a modest house on a street a block from the church and grocery store. They had no car, their entire back yard a garden. To them, this was *everything*.

I was just five, starting kindergarten, when they moved from the farm. But before that, I remember the sweet smell of the milking barn and hayloft, the sound of the gravel crunching under the tires, the crayon colors of grass and buttercups that formed a strip in the middle of the lane. Also the pansies with their purple faces along the front of the little white house. I see gladiolas blushing by a gate, although I can't be sure if there was a gate. If there was, it would have most certainly been open. Marigolds bordered each of my grandmother's gardens: first on the farm, then in their backyard in town, the orange bunches not a boundary meant to keep children out. My grandmother planted marigolds in her garden to avoid the use of pesticides.

~

In the Old Country, as my grandparents called it, the borders changed over the span of my ancestors' lives, German-speaking settlers, Mennonites, who arrived in the fertile land near Warsaw, a lowland region, as early as 1750 or 1760 from the Danzig area, now Gdansk. Before them, Dutch Mennonites came to Poland as early as 1528. Considered heretics by Catholic and Protestant authorities, these Anabaptists migrated from the Low Countries and settled along areas of the Vistula River, establishing "Hollander" villages. In 1642, the Polish King gave these agrarian people special privileges for settling here. As the land became occupied, their descendants proceeded south, and from there into the interior of Poland.

During the late eighteenth century, Mennonites established the settlements of Deutsch Kazun and Deutsch Wymyschle[2] near Warsaw, the home of my ancestors, as well as other settlements. But the Polish Kingdom, stretching from the Baltic to the Black Sea, was portioned between three other kingdoms, Russia, Austria, and Prussia, and for over one hundred years—from 1795 to 1918—Poland disappeared.

My grandfather was born in 1900, my grandmother in 1903. At the time my grandparents were born, their birthplace was part of Russia. Those living in my grandparents' village, Deutsch Wymyschle were of Flemish origin, from Flanders, now Belgium. Many of the village settlers were also Frisian, from Holland. My grandmother's ancestors, the Kliewers, which means "dwellers among the clover," were Mennonites of Frisian descent. Her grandparents were Heinrich and Maria Kliewer. Their son, Kornelius, would be orphaned at age twelve, and later would become my grandmother's father.

My grandfather's side is from the family of the Count von Schroeter, county of Hildesheim, Germany. A son, Wilhelm Schroeter, (my grandfather's great-great-grandfather?) fled Hildesheim during the Napoleonic wars at the beginning of the French Revolutionary wars (around 1789), and was robbed of all his money and possessions by his servants, so it has been told. Schroeter came to the Mennonites in Prussia, and from there, to Deutsch Wymyschle, Poland. Schroeter remained "of Lutheran faith," which might suggest why the brand of Mennonite on my mother's side seemed more "worldly" than the more pious Mennonites in the village. For example, my grandfather was not a preacher, deacon, choir director, Bible or Sunday school teacher in a village where life was centered on the church, the family, the farm. I'm not even sure he went to church until later in life.

---

2. German spelling of the village in Poland.

He even smoked tobacco, and drank alcohol (but he would give up those vices in Canada). My grandmother, I am told, had, in the memories of her little children, always kept the faith. As a grandchild I knew her to be an encourager, open-hearted, without judgment, generous, and a dedicated reader of the Scriptures.

As for my grandfather's family, the record of lineage has been so far traced back to my grandfather's father, David Schroeder, who died when my grandfather was two years old, and to his grandfather, Jakob, and his great-grandfather David (1796–1855). It's possible then, that the German Count came before him, but his name was not recorded in the Mennonite church records because he was not born a Mennonite.

Thus, perhaps Count Wilhelm begat David, David begat Jakob, Jakob begat David, and David begat Wilhelm (my grandfather). But my grandfather and his older sister, from the ages of two and four, were raised by their mother's second husband, a man named Ratzlaff, also from the village. The origin of the name Ratzlaff is uncertain. It may be of Polish/Slavic origin.[3] There is also the thought that all Mennonites with this surname stem from a Swedish soldier who passed through the village. According to a relative, Eric L. Ratzlaff, who chronicled the history of the village, it seems the soldier stayed. Stopping by the church, he heard the pastor speak. "He was influenced by the sermons he heard and wanted to join the congregation. He was moved to withdraw his sword from its sheath and thrust it into a hedgepost."[4] He also fell in love with the pastor's daughter. It's a good story.

During World War I (1914–1918), according to his own handwritten *aufzeichnungen* (which means notes, or record), my grandfather served four years in the 10th Artillery Regiment of the Polish Army as a gunner in the battle against the Bolsheviks. Pacifism was no longer considered a core tenet of the faith by all Mennonites. Poland became an independent country again during the inter-war period, 1919–1939. The Second World War began when the country was invaded by Nazi Germany and the Soviet Union. It was occupied by Germany during the war, but remained under the dominion of the Soviet Union when the war ended. When my grandparents tried to leave with their children in front of the Red Army, January 1945, it was too late. With my grandfather taken prisoner, my mother remembers that her mother and the children were the only remaining family from the community during that time. Left behind. Both Polish historians

---

3. Peters and Thiessen, *Mennonitische Namen*, 105.
4. Ratzlaff, *From the Don to the Fraser*, 2.

and scholars of Mennonite history have claimed that in 1945 the Mennonite population virtually disappeared from Poland.

When my grandparents finally immigrated to Canada in 1951, a border around their painful memories was also erected, a silent wall. Even so, they embodied an elsewhere. I touched it when I hugged them; it was in their dress, my grandfather's woolen shirts, trousers, and suspenders, a cap or hat to shade his eyes, and in my grandmother's simple dresses, her apron and kerchief to cover her head. More deeply, their hands, thick from farm labor, aged with blue veins, were like tributaries of blood through a Polish village. This elsewhere was also evident in their heavily accented and few halting English words, but their mouths a free-flowing faucet of Low German, *Plaut Dietsch*, a dialect that derived from the Netherlands and developed in Poland's Vistula delta—translated as "flat Deutsch/German—Diets/Dutch" and more precisely, as "ordinary language." This language was one of the ways the Mennonite people kept their identity. A language I cannot speak, though I still understand a few words, an intimate cadence of foreign words calling to mind my grandparents.

⌒

Like my grandmother's crochet—snowflake-patterned handiwork of patience—story requires time, often a lifetime. And this is the silent mystery that descends; each life is connected to other lives, past, present, and future.

⌒

It is 4:45 in the afternoon on August 18th, 2005, and we—my husband, three children, my parents, and I—have crossed the border into Poland. We've traveled from Dresden, and after departing the rebuilt city, moving eastward along the rail line, we see the deterioration, the crumbling buildings, brick canvases for the scrawl of graffiti giving way to the countryside as the train covers the kilometers of our journey. At a small station, after a series of jolts and the clamor of heavy steel on rail we have dropped the first train car. Our car becomes the one directly behind the locomotive as we now jerk our way past small weathered houses with huge gardens and fruit trees. Further along the tracks, we pass by small garden houses adjacent to the tracks where, on this sunny late afternoon, families—parents, children, grandparents—sit in plastic chairs after hoeing, weeding, or pulling up vegetables, as they watch the train roll past on its way to Warsaw.

On the seat across from me, my mother, who at this time is sixty-six, unfolds a paper, a hand-drawn map of her village, taken from her travel purse. Her older brother Henry had drawn it after some of the siblings had come back to see the Old Country. He has sent it along with her so she can show us the old home place. It has been almost sixty years since her family's abrupt departure; their uprooting.

My parents are exchanging the few Polish words they begin to recall from the time I've known so little about. It's interesting to hear them although I don't know what they're saying. Perhaps only conversational phrases—"Hello. What is your name?" My father is from Ukraine and has childhood memories of clashing armies, refugee life in Dresden before the bombing, then in Yugoslavia and Austria. He must have picked up a few Polish phrases during or after the war. These foreign words, buried beneath their second language, English, are like small shoots poking out of this soil.

We are passing through a forest of oak, birch, and tall, slim pines with reddish bark. I recall the forests of my childhood's thick *Grimm's Fairy Tale Book*, the one in German. In the stories, forests always lined the edge of what was familiar, the border between the Known and the Unknown. The Unknown, at once mysterious and ominous, entailed witches, ogres, and children in stories about cruelty and overcoming adversity.

As we travel further into Poland toward Warsaw, we pass a woman, a headscarf tied over her hair in the manner of my grandmother when she worked in her garden or kitchen. The woman is watching her cows graze. The pastures are arranged in stripes, yellow and green, which my children, who learned this in high school geography, explain to me might be crop rotation. Farming in thin strips is a way of controlling the pests without pesticides and it also prevents soil erosion. In one field I see hay, rolled into neat spools. In another the farmer has mounded the hay onto a tall pole and I see what haystacks, such as those in the land of fairy-tales, really look like.

We roll past cornfields. Behind them are stands of pine and fir. It is hay and corn season here, just like at home in the Fraser Valley. Through the train window I see the sun begin to lower over the fields, heightening the beige and yellow hues of the hay, the yarrow and the silky crowns on the corn stalks. Thin trunks of pine trees flush orange in the background and the golden light glints like fire from the windows of the simple farmhouses.

Black-and-white milk cows chew grass before their evening milking.

There is sandy soil among the forests, white roads of sand threading through this plain. One road runs parallel to the tracks, a strip of green weeds where the car tires don't roll, and I am reminded of the driveway to my grandparents' plain clapboard farmhouse. Though it was less than twenty miles to their house from ours, as a small child the ride seemed as long as my present train ride from this point on to Warsaw, now an hour away by rail.

I wonder if some of the brown stripes we roll past are potato patches. My grandmother always planted potatoes in her garden. She'd serve us bowlfuls of small new potatoes with sweet yellow flesh we children called "Polish potatoes," best with only butter and salt.

On the sandy road beside the rails, I see an old man in a cap riding a rickety bicycle to a patch where a cow is grazing. I remember that my grandfather wore a cap like that.

Further on, a woman in a dark red dress and blue head scarf walks through her square of earth. She carries a metal pail. Judging by her gait it looks heavy, perhaps filled with newly-dug potatoes. Small puffs rise after each footfall and particles of dirt light up with evening glow.

Pine forests turn to beech forests. The train has slowed to a stop. It is 7:35 pm and we must be approaching the suburbs of Warsaw.

～

During our stay in Warsaw we will walk to the historic center and visit the site of the ghetto. The city was razed by the Nazis after the uprising of the ghetto in 1944. Warsaw has been rebuilt, and the Old Town exists today as it once did almost to the nail and cobblestone, reconstructed from paintings painted before the partitions of Poland in the late eighteenth century, about the time my German-speaking ancestors established their village near Warsaw. It is mystifying and consoling how the human spirit endeavors to rebuild itself.

Just as mystifying is the way that place can pull the body to itself, just as north pulls the needle of a compass. Homeplace is a magnetic field. My mother reminded me that her father came back to the village in the summer of 1973, over two decades following the war's aftermath and after the darkness, but while Poland was under Communist rule.

I didn't know it then, but just before this time, in 1970, then-West German chancellor, Willy Brandt, traveled to Poland on a State visit, and knelt in silence before a monument at the Warsaw Ghetto. Then, only eight years old, I wouldn't have known what had happened here although I knew my grandparents and parents had lived through the war. But my world was still small, and in it, my family, the Canadian town where we lived. Not yet the past.

~

Poland was home for the Jews in Diaspora. In her book, *Shtetl*, Eva Hoffman writes that for many centuries, before the war, Poland was home to the largest Jewish population in the world.[5] And here Polish Jewry gave rise to Yiddish and Hebrew culture.[6]

The name Poland was pronounced Polania, shortened to Polin. The word *polin* in Hebrew means, "Here you shall rest."

By 1592, there were many Calvinists and Lutherans in Poland, but the most numerous of the religious groups were the Jews, and the entire Polish trade was in their hands.[7] Those Jews, not well-off, were the tailors, cobblers, carpenters, blacksmiths, and tinkers.

My mother's village, founded in 1762, lies approximately one hundred kilometers west of Warsaw. The Mennonite colonists built the first village church here in 1813. The village was home to other German-speaking colonists and co-religionists—Lutherans and Baptists. No Jewish people lived among them in the farming village.

~

In her preschool memory, my mother's village had seemed isolated from what began to happen at the onset of occupation by Germany, although my mother tells me that in her kindergarten class, the children, age five, were required to say "Heil Hitler," arm out stiff in salute. The older children attended compulsory youth groups. The girls in higher grades wore the navy jumpers of their group. In the village, flapping in the yard of every house, a flag, red with the black cross in a white circle. In the village classroom, and in each home hung a photograph of Adolf Hitler.

My mother remembers that her parents used to go to the neighboring town, Gabin (in German it was Gombin) seven kilometers from her village,

5. Hoffman, *Shtetl*, 2.
6. Ibid., 8
7. Ibid., 49.

where her mother ordered matching dresses sewn by a tailor. The six girls, Martha and Anna, Emilie and Erna, and Ella and Tilly were dressed as matching pairs. My mother, Erna, now on the train rolling towards her early childhood, recalls a maroon coat and hat.

Gabin had one of Poland's oldest and grandest wooden synagogues, built in 1710, and for centuries the town was home to a large Jewish population. At the time my mother was born, Polish Jews, Catholics, and Christians, including Mennonites, lived harmoniously in Gabin.

"On one visit to the tailor, he and his wife were simply gone," my mother says now, this memory of her four-year-old self like a loosened thread from the maroon coat.

"Each spring gypsies used to set up camp in the fields of Wymyschle with their wagons, but they stopped coming during the German occupation," she comments.

She tells us people came through their village to ask for food; I wonder if she means those who fled advancing troops or were displaced. She said that my grandmother always gave something to anyone who came to the door. She would not have had much to give, but she grew a garden. She baked bread. In her last years in the care home, she always gave me a parting gift, a cookie, a candy.

∿

Why did I come in the summer of 2005 with my mother, father, and family? The best answer I can give for the trip, at the time, was I wanted to know where I had come from, at once a geography of the self and a landscape of otherness. At the time, other questions were yet to appear, like the potato seeds my grandmother took away with her when she fled her home and abandoned her garden with a hope they would later grow in new soil.

My unformed questions were the seeds that now seek the shape of words. They say you can keep seeds for a long, long time. Then, no matter how long they are kept, when placed into ground, they will germinate. In the same manner, from their silence my words grow into story.

∿

August 19th 2005, we have hired a van and driver to take us to my mother's former village. We are off the main highway driving through the countryside on another bumpy road, old asphalt over cobblestones. Mountain ash trees with orange berries line the road. We pass cucumber fields. Yellow rapeseed grows along the roadside. There are many small farms, each cut into five hectares from once larger estates, now remnants from Communist times. The trunks of the poplar trees are thick from the Vistula River (the *Weichsel* as it was known to my family) which is very close. Near its banks are summer homes or *dachas* with gardens.

A stork flies past the van. Two more white storks stand on the rooftop of a house. On one side of the road a farmer has placed a basket on a pole for a stork to roost. On the other side of the road at another farm, a stork has built its own nest. In September the native storks will migrate from Poland to Africa and Egypt.

Sklep. Store. They sell candy, *zukerki*.

They sell the soft milk candies that my grandmother always gave out to the grandchildren each Christmas when I was small. Funk's Supermarket, a Mennonite family-owned grocery store in our town, sold these sweets, imported from Poland. We called them Polish candies. We've stopped at the *sklep* to buy bottles of water and to park the van so we can walk to the river. From here we will scramble over the dike to reach the water, running swiftly. We will not get too close because of the standing water along the bank. The roar of the rapids blends with the breeze through the giant willow trees. Birds chirp.

We pass a woman hoeing, harvesting potatoes, *kartoffel sammlung*, which reminds my mother of her seven-year-old self as a homeless refugee, shaking out potatoes, separating the large ones from the small ones.

We cross the bridge of a smaller river. A tributary sparkles, as if a child has sprinkled silver glitter onto blue paper. Wooden hay wagons stand in fields awaiting modern square bales to transport to barns. My mother, daughter, and I sit down in the tall grass speckled with purple wild flowers and lean into one another for a photograph. When I look at it now, it appears we are surfacing through ripples of grass.

Plodz. A town along the way. "My mother used to talk about this place when I was small," my own mother remembers as we pass the road sign. "My parents must have known people here," she says. We drive on, past a sunflower field, and my mother now remembers her family had one too; all these small details I've never heard her mention before. We pass apple orchards. Petrakowitz, another town my mother suddenly remembers. Her parents had friends here, she explains.

Beyond the strips of grass, corn, rapeseed, we see a sign, *Wymysle–5 km*! W is pronounced V; S is pronounced *sh*. There is a Wymysle *Polski*, but we are going to *Nowo* Wymysle, formerly *Deutsch* Wymyschle.

Nowo Wymysle: We pull the van over and cluster around the sign for a photograph, three generations of us. From the sign, a narrow and dusty white road leads us through a pine forest and when we pass through the road crooks right and unrolls like a ribbon through the village. We park the van in the first driveway at the end of the road that has led us here. The building on the yard is made of planks over a hundred years old, and though my mother doesn't recognize it at first, it happens to be my mother's kindergarten. This will be our starting point.

A couple with a small child lives inside the old log one-room kindergarten which looks more like a shed. The young man and his wife are child-like themselves; perhaps about twenty years old. He is outgoing and friendly, and she is shy. Both smile widely, proud of their toddler, as he motions for us to enter the dim interior where, through a small window coated with dirt, a thin lance of sunlight slices through the dark. We peer into the doorway and step inside for a moment. The woman from next door comes over to see who we are. She is the mother of the young man, the grandmother of the child. She wears a polka-dotted dress with an apron tied over it. She tells us she has lived here since 1946, after all the German-speaking villagers were gone.

～

From age four through nine, about the period of 1943 to 1948, my mother's memories are a winter's heavy sky. Silence like a thick snowfall; it is insulating and isolating. Time and silence helps to bear suffering. For a time. And then, any sorrow can be borne if a story can be told about it—words that have been attributed to the Danish author Karen Blixen.

My mother tries to orient herself with her map, but the kindergarten has been left off. From here we will walk to the other end of the village where the family home site will be. Further down the road, I see a wooden house barn, the style of house with an attached barn from a former era of my mother's childhood, the yard surrounded by an unpainted wooden picket fence. All the wood silvered by weather and age. The houses are situated on one side, the fields and the pine forest through which we came, on the other.

The road is a light sand road that sends up puffs when we walk.

It is a small village but all the landmarks of my mother's early life remain, though what is here is more like the shadow cast by what once was.

A Mennonite church had been established here in 1813, but the building burnt down in the 1850s. It was rebuilt in the 1860s, and remains as the simple church that is still standing; its plaster falling off to expose the bricks. This is the church my grandparents were married in, November 24th, 1923. The floor of the inside is dirt now, the structure is empty. It hasn't been used as a church since the War.

A little farther along we come to a cemetery among the trees. In a former time it was a cleared site and well-kept, but now it looks forgotten. There are no gravestones, only trees. Beyond the trees the grass grows tall. But among the dry grass my husband has found a grave site, an old flat stone with the name *Schroeder*. He scrapes off the moss to see it better. It is of Matilda Kliewer *geboren* (born) *Schroeder, 25 Oktober___, gestorben* (died) *1931*. This woman was likely related to my grandfather, and married a man related to my grandmother. The marker bears my mother's paternal and maternal family names. My grandfather, a Schroeder, and my grandmother, a Kliewer. However, as in ethnic communities and rural villages of a former time, both my grandparents' families had surnames in common; my grandmother's father was a Kliewer, and my grandfather's mother, Anna, was a Kliewer, though she was buried in Olds, Alberta in 1966. It is likely this woman buried in Poland, turned to dust, her marker barely legible, is related to either, and both.

Both my grandparents have been gone for decades now, but my grandmother was born in this village in 1903, the fifth and last child to Kornelius Kliewer (the miller) and his wife, Jacobine. When her mother died in childbirth, she grew up as an only child in her Aunt Pauline's and Uncle Heinrich's house, though she had older siblings, Emilie, Peter, Albertine, Wilhelmine, and Mathilde. Kornelius remarried (his late wife's sister Wilhelmine) and had five more children. *Babtjche*, the widowed and aged aunt always lived with my grandparents and my mother remembers as a small child, sleeping with *Babtjche* to keep her warm. *Babtjche* died when my mother was five.

I suspect at one time, there were markers bearing many of these names except for my grandparents, my grandmother's older sisters, and

Kornelius—those who had immigrated to Canada. Perhaps my grandparents' infant son Peter, their second child, born March 13th, 1926, was buried here. Though not their first-born, David; the death notice had stated, Saporoschje, Ukraine, October 25th, 1943.

It is peaceful here among the trees, leaves rustling in the light wind.

We come upon the former school building, now abandoned; there is a separate red brick building on the yard that my mother remembers was used for drying the herbs that the older girls learned to gather. These were used for medicinal purposes which the occupying German army shipped back for use in Germany. During the capitulation in 1945, German children no longer were permitted to attend school. My mother had turned six. It occurs to me my mother did not receive an education until she came to Canada years later.

In the school yard, my mother used to herd the cow and geese for the school teacher.

Nearby is the pond.

Next to the school is the family home site. The house is gone. From the photo my mother has that survived, a photo of the family taken on the yard in front of the house, only the wide planks are visible.

How strange to think that the land is the same land as then, the foundation of their home. The home first of the childless Heinrich and Paulina, then after my grandparents married, the home each of their children were born in. It is now an overgrown field. Here too are mushrooms the size of dinner plates. And two old acacia trees with patterned bark mark the place. My mother remembers the trees.

Like all the farms, theirs was a strip of ten acres. Some of the land lay in front of the house, across the road. Here the crops were sown, wheat, hay, potatoes, the only suitable crops because the soil is very sandy. There is nothing grown here now, save for the hay. Poverty is evident in this village in 2005.

And in a previous time, the forest was further back. The pines and birch have long begun their steady advance toward the road.

~

We've come to the end of the road, but before we turn around we walk to the swimming hole in pastureland behind the houses. Here the brothers, my uncles, swam. The swimming hole is murky, shallow, filled in with grass.

I hear crickets, watch butterflies flutter, bow to pluck a strand of wild forget-me-knots and buttercups, and place the petals between the pages of the notebook I have brought. What more can I carry away with me?

In his book, *Native Realm*, Czeslaw Milosz writes, "It is incredible how much of the aura of a country can penetrate a child. Stronger than thought is an image—dry leaves on a path, of twilight, of heavy sky."[8] On this day in the sunshine, I try to imagine my mother's early life, a turbulent time she finds difficult to retrieve. She prefers to draw from memory's calmer moments. This day, as we walk through her old village, she says she remembers the feel of the road in summer on her bare feet; of playing in the sand; her mother's garden; walking down to the far end of the road on the first day of kindergarten.

It is the pure moments, the simple joys a young child tucks away, like a smooth stone from the streambed, a talisman in her pocket to rub. The sharper stones left behind, mitigated by time—these stones I will bend to collect.

On this August afternoon in 2005, as we return to the van parked on the sandy road, I notice the trail of foot prints we had left earlier, and I recognize my own shoes.

---

8. Milosz, *Native Realm*, 45.

3

Nothing but Words

I think our memories, beautiful and traumatic, are the inchoate, incessant demands for meaning we reach for, approach, and come near to, but never conclusively arrive at. Perhaps this is what memory and faith hold in common. When my mother asked me to tell the story of her childhood in Poland, I began to write poems about the memories I had of my maternal grandparents. My mother's memories of war were difficult to talk about. "I wish to trust poetry," writes the poet and memoirist Patricia Hampl, in her collection *I Could Tell You Stories*. Though it is made of "nothing but words," poetry, she says, not only represents our *lived life*, but *the veiled existence of the soul*.[1] I think I, too, have wished to write poetry about past lives and loss, for this reason. And perhaps because, as Hampl adds, poetry is capable of religious revelation in ways religion is not.

In my mind, my grandparents had always been old. They embodied an intelligible weariness, despite my grandmother's remarkable industriousness and optimistic nature well into old age. My grandfather was amiable, affectionate to young children, and, when they moved off the farm to the little house in town, was what may truthfully be characterized as indolent. Long after he died, a relative recounted that when he had once asked my grandfather why he wasn't much interested in acquiring things, or "getting ahead," my grandfather had replied, "What for? It will only be taken away again." Also noted by others about my grandfather was he was not an

1. Hampl. *I Could Tell You Stories*, 152.

envious man. He was content. At the time my grandfather had purportedly said this—was it at age sixty or seventy?—sometime after starting over in Canada in his late fifties, he may have been thinking about end-of-life matters. But no doubt, this was a reference to the times he had endured, the devastating loss of a way of life and homeplace in war. Displacement.

My grandparents never spoke to me about their dead son, and I don't know if they spoke about him with others either. Nonetheless, I sensed in their absence of words that, over time, they continued to mourn a lost child in private and quiet ways. Behind the closed door, in the spare bedroom, where my grandmother sometimes sewed, the face of their son as a child peered out from a frame—grey monochromatic tones from the faded past. When I was in elementary school, I observed them as I visited them one Remembrance Day, a poppy pinned to my sweater. That morning, they quietly left the kitchen closing the bedroom door behind them. I observed the long minute hand of the electric clock in the kitchen as it ticked out a full rotation, second by second. Time seemed to lengthen, and then the clock in the front room chimed 11:00 at last.

It seems I have loved my grandparents longer than I can remember. Perhaps even before I was born—is such a thing possible? My parents lived on a little farm next to theirs when my mother was pregnant with me, then our young family moved to another farm my parents bought, but on the same small prairie, not too far away. Throughout their remaining lives, in the house in town, at the end in the care home, I lived near them. As foreign as they were in Canada, never fluent in the language their grandchildren spoke, they embodied for us a dwelling place; they gathered us to them, the grandchildren and children of immigrants, and we were at home.

While most of the poems I have written bear my own memories, I also began to imagine my mother's and her family's lives before my time, and wrote poems about that. The spaces between lines seemed appropriate as I considered the setting of my grandparents in the Polish countryside and the time of my mother's childhood, until she was nine, in Poland. I trusted poetry to be permeable so that what I imagined was not fiction, and in the spaces, the unsaid, unspoken truths existed. I trusted it to bear the compression of her family's experience I had not experienced, the white space carrying the weight. Poems, I understood, would not require chronology, dates, or artifacts and documents to verify their meaning. I could weave back and forth, through time, move to and fro geographically, or in circles around the givens. Circumambulate, hint, suggest, and tell a truth. Writing about my mother's family, and of their life in Poland conjured up turmoil. My heritage of German-speaking colonists of a Pacifist sect, was a motor through muddy water. The paradox of intimacy and silence unfolded; line and space, light and dark, zenith and nadir. Perhaps paradox is why intuitively I pursued poetry.

Only afterwards, after I had completed, polished, and published the poetry, I noticed an interesting phenomenon, a strange mirroring from the murky water of the past. Many of the poems arose from memories of early consciousness, my four- and five-year-old self, perhaps my most carefree time. This time was permeated with the presence of my grandparents, and I, the same age my mother had been when she experienced the personally traumatic and life-altering events of World War II—full of the presence of death and an atmosphere of fear. The loss of a brother, a failed refugee flight, a father and their home taken from them.

My aunt Ella, my mother's younger sister, has told me her earliest conscious memories are over-ridden by this sensation of fear. Though my mother hardly speaks of it, she remembers being taken, at age six, from her mother. All *Volksdeutsch*, including children deemed old enough, were dispersed to farms as labor. A young child has no language for such experiences. Sadly, those silent or silenced memories are not forgotten, but remain hidden and painful wounds.[2] Poland was the site of this child's earliest memory, of belonging and family. Poland, during my mother's young life, was also the epicenter of the last century's destruction, and the site of a contested national memory.

As a student of literature I learned that many language theorists, philosophers, and poets point out that the very act of writing a story, a poem, is a moral act. In her essay, "Czeslaw Milosz and Memory," Patricia Hampl points out that for Milosz, the Lithuanian-born Polish Nobel Laureate who witnessed the destruction of Poland, the purpose of lyric poetry and memoir was both personal and historical, not merely that of a storyteller, but as a witness. And in this way, memory is "the tabernacle of human experience."[3] Milosz held that the poet's work is to affirm life.[4] "What is poetry which does not save / nations or people?" Milosz, a Catholic, had written from Warsaw in 1945, in his poem "Dedication."[5] It is true Milosz spoke for his

2. Ricoeur, *Memory History Forgetting*, 445.

3. Hampl, *I Could Tell You Stories*, 98.

4 Nathan and Quinn, *The Poet's Work*, 87.

5. Milosz, *Selected Poems*, 1931–2004, 39.

generation, a voice for the many, acknowledging a world in ruins in the face of genocide, but as a poet he was also speaking out in resistance to Theodore Adorno's notion that poetry, like God, was, if not dead, then impotent to renew life.

Hampl writes about her Czech grandmother, and of her own quest for her Czech heritage, in her book, *A Romantic Education*. In it, she makes an observation that has also made an impression on me. Though Hampl is already third-generation, she says someone born immediately after the Second World War—or anyone born after 1945 (she was born in 1945)—has a sense of being born into an elegy.[6] And it is true, in my case, that children born after seek to understand its lingering effects, its shaping influences even as its survivors are dying.

Some of my mother's recollections might be from her earliest consciousness: for example, the abrupt memory of a maroon coat and visit to the Jewish tailor when she must have been three years old. Suddenly, on the train to Warsaw at age sixty-six, the memory rises to the surface. Or they might be the recollections of her mother, or an older sister, passed on to her, too young to remember or to have been present. All the same, a memory has clung, and demands significance. It is a marker along our journey.

Memory is a frayed chord. Memories of memories, the cord frays further. But, for someone like me, is this distance in time as ominous as a break from the past? I suspect not, if I pay attention to both words and silences.

Is memory more like ripples in water? From a stone, the ripples widen around it, these rings mere traces of the stone, memories of the stone, widening out, until the water is completely still.

Then we drop another stone.

My mother's story hasn't let go of me. It is not that I have a fascination with a particular place in Poland, my mother's small agrarian village a hundred kilometers from Warsaw, as Hampl confesses her fascination with her ancestral city, Prague. To her, that iconic city serves as the representation of a history the post-war generation is living out of, a past she points out we thought we were done with. "This history is like the long, reverberating chime from a cathedral bell," she writes, "which moves through the air by

6. Hampl, *A Romantic Education*, 175.

feel, by vibration, rather than by actual sound, long after the tone itself has dissipated, and everyone assumes there is silence."[7]

Although the poems I wrote are simply those of a daughter and grand-daughter of the first generation to be born in the new world, they were my attempts to witness lives that were affected in silent and lingering ways; these poems like widening circles of movement. At first, I wrote poems about my own early memories which led me to write about a deeper past.

Perhaps the process of taking a closer look at the past is more aptly represented in the image of rings of a tree; unseen, a record of life, visible only when a cross section is taken, or the tree cut down. The past has been like this for me. Poetry has always been a way of dealing with the emotional realities of the past, a desire to be truthful—that yearning for meaning-making in a world where there is senseless violence and stunning beauty.

7. Ibid., 174.

Polished Buttons

On visits to my grandmother's house when I was five,
I remember taking—as if leftover buttons shining
in the mason jar beside her treadle machine

in the spare bedroom—glances at the photograph
of a child, no longer living,
and not meant for me to talk about. Sometimes,

when my grandmother was preoccupied,
cooking up a pot of borscht in the kitchen, I would steal
into her sewing room and stare at her boy,

or I would press my foot to the Singer's peddle,
humming a line of invisible stitches to far-away,
where she came from. One time, I tucked

my head into the living room, curious as to why she was lying
on the couch in the middle of the day. This seemed odd,
she was usually in the kitchen kneading dough, or in the garden

hoeing and I knew something was wrong. I was too young
to know the word *cancer*, my mother and aunt whispering.
That must have been when I first learned to tuck away

pain like a polished button in the pocket
of my grandmother's apron. She lived on, and as I grew older
I understood that she was content not to story me

with stitches of loss, although I wanted details
of her life to fasten her to me forever. So, near the end,
each time I visited her in the care home, I left
with so many questions.

Home is in the evening shade of a low mountain.

Buttercups grow between the strips of gravel road.
Crunch of the tires,
swish of the grass
under the floor boards; this is the song the car sings
as it carries a small child
toward the old farmhouse
with the green trim and the screen door.

Behind the modest white house, a wash line
grows from the yard
near the garden and the raspberry patch
stretches out towards the slope of the mountain.

It's always summer in memory,
unless it's Christmas together with all the cousins
gathered around the evergreen.

In the garden bordered with marigolds
we grandchildren wander freely
among bean stalks and potatoes,

rows and rows planted
after all those years of a family's displacement,
gorging on plucked carrots,
unwashed, dark earth clinging to the corners of our mouths.

Soil is the taste of belonging.

And language is the heart's true home place.
There were low mountains there. Did this river valley
call to mind the Vistula? *Die gute alte Heimat,* Home
Sweet Home. By the age of two, I spoke
their words for food and rest and family.
Named them with endearments, *Oma, Opa.*
Syllables and sound of first-language
flowed from my tongue like honey, child-like

sweetness to pour over their unspoken loss.

I return to the place
long after they both have died,
after even my own children are grown.
I follow the road towards the low mountain
wanting to collect my memories.
The raspberry fields and the house are gone
—still, I know where to go.

Memory longs for the journey
just as the body longs
for its own ground.

The Place of Memory

Memory resides in the house
of my body. Does memory

also inhabit the land? Does it
flow like blood and river

through the heart? After they're gone,

those I love dwell
in memory–

but what of those forgotten

memories,
theirs, too painful to unearth,

buried in the ground of Elsewhere;
in the past of Then?

History is a silent country.

What a Grandfather Leaves

Scent of peppermint on his breath,

click of candy against his teeth,
those he left by the sink in a glass
and we grandchildren would laugh.
His chuckle almost inaudible,
low quake and belly shake.

He didn't leave words, he had only few
he could speak in a language he'd never master,
we, forgetting his tongue each year we grew older.
Him, at the table, pointing his finger
at food our grandmother made,
sign-language for us to pass the bowl. "Thank you,"
words he could say for potatoes boiled soft
and the gravy fat she spooned over.

He had starved during the war. A prisoner,
gone years, he came back all sagging skin
over bones, loose teeth and the youngest, a baby
when father was taken—the family displaced—
confused as to why mother was laughing
and crying at once for the gaunt stranger

who had searched for and found them.
She loved him for surviving. He returned,
but never the same, his leg wouldn't heal.
Diabetes later, those cravings,
filling his pockets, palming Scotch Mints
like marbles or coins, or crumbs of bread, rationed.

Evenings he'd sit, she washing
his feet, blue, and still-open sore.
She wordlessly bound all his wounds;
they spoke of them no more. Their vows
sacred despite separation. And when we asked them

to kiss, he'd pursue her, she clucking protests,
then lips pursed, they'd peck just for us

and we'd shriek in delight at the old pair
with false teeth. How he teased her
in front of us, why must she fuss so,
and we'd snicker as he dished candy out
by the pocket-full just before dinner, and him,
crawling along her swept linoleum,
we in the sway of our faithful old horse,

his bad back. Was he remembering the draught horse,
muscled and brown, pulling the wagon,
ploughing the soil he loved so? He loved her,

my grandmother, because *she* was the strong one.
She was the one who gave him
the will to go on, the only one
who could nag him as they started over
without money or home, but the riches
of children still living. We loved him
though we were simply too young

to truly have known him—in the village
in Poland, the stern father, his vices;
she burdened with chores of farm
and church-going neighbors'
heads shaking. Our grandfather from afar
where fighting regimes claimed all he had owned,

but here, familiar round belly-laughter,
suspenders holding pants up
to his chest, full of gratitude, straw hat
shading those faded blue eyes
looking into the sun. In front of their house
unfolding his chair. I still see him. How he'd wait

for our visits, his children's children, his tribe

in this land, offer us sweets, hug us close
and rub our cheeks with his stubble—so close,

I can almost catch the peppermint scent of his breath.

My Grandmother's Strong Name

For Jacobine

I.
The door ajar, you were always open-hearted.

My footsteps slowed before your room—the entrance
framed you like a photograph.

Before you could hear me, I saw you,
your outline, white-haired in the filtered light,

seated at your reading table by the window, your Bible
open, and that day's meditation from "The Daily Bread."

You sensed me watching you through the gap—
I'll always see you this way.

II.
Frailty belies strength. At ninety, you had lived
a life large enough to give birth to twelve children,
bury an infant, and grieve your first-born,

without a gravestone on the Russian front
only a letter bore his name;

large enough to have lost a homeland in,
and gained another. Such expansiveness
your small room holds. Bare, but for your Bible

and wind-up clock to mark time.

Twenty years more you lived after his stroke.
I was a young bride then. You a widow,
taught me much about vows.

Nun-like with your Bible, praying daily for us
in your room, enlarged by your contentment
in small things—cookies and tea
with a grandchild who'd come to visit,
and verses. These were your treasures on earth.

You were never one to hold on
to possessions. You held us all

loosely with bonds fine as your lacework,
three and four generations intertwined
after all the migrations.

III.
From *Wiaczemin*, your people settled here while you remained,
a young mother, pregnant again, though the reason for staying
was *Babtjche*, too old to leave—or to leave her. *Nor would you.*
Barren, she raised you from birth, when your own mother died.

History redraws the borders, but where
does the beginning end and ending begin
if the land is not the same
our ancestors are born of and buried in?

IV.
A current pulls from the Carpathians
through Warsaw. The river Vistula in late winter,
1945; my mother has never forgotten the crossing.

Turned back at the border, armed soldiers
pressing in, forced over the thaw, black water
rising above the river's ice skin to her ankles—
she didn't break through. But can you imagine,
she asks me now, what a mother goes through?

Beneath the groans of ice, I can almost hear
silent fear, you praying for the other shore.

After the capture, you were relegated from citizen
to village wash-woman, hands as raw as your heart,
youngest children crying with hunger, older ones

taken and scattered. And you walked hours to Warsaw
bringing bread to the prisoner behind the barbed wire.

As a hen gathers her chicks, you sought each one. Foot-sore,
you led them to refuge where he found you at war's end.

V.
Small grandmother of Dutch-German origin,
with your strong name in feminine form,

you were named after Jacob, the one who wrestled
with God for a blessing. How you would wrestle with life.

We are the blessed ones, born here,
because you gathered your children.

VI.
Your door ajar, I entered your life.
You belonged to elsewhere;
at the same time, you belonged to me.

When I was a child, at the approach of our car,
you, knowing its sound, the way the cow, milk-heavy,
her calf, rushed from the kitchen, pushing open
the screen door even before we had parked;

wiping your thick hands on your apron,
pulling off your headscarf . . . .

As I grew older, we had no particular conversations.
I mostly watched the way you enjoyed
family around you, preparing meals we devoured,

serving until your hands thinned,

vellum paper-skinned.
When I looked in, your eyes
blurred behind bifocals, a line
dividing all that you had seen
into the past and the future.

My eyes are the color yours were.

As I see it, you lived as if you had always known
your suffering, and your joy, would be great—not asking *why*
along the length of temporality's unfolding shadow.

My inheritance is your unspoken words.

The Yard—August 19, 2005

(after *Meadow*, Czeslaw Milosz)

The Vistula runs alongside the meadows,
the fields lush before the harvest,
hay wagons stand ready
for bales to fill old barns and lofts.

We had a map. Walking past fields,
the sand road billowing under our feet
we found it—
green grasses and wild flowers
growing where the house once stood.

Where? Where exactly, the house?
We couldn't say, but we knew
this empty yard was the ground
of my mother's childhood.

With eyes half-closed
against that afternoon August sun,
in the stillness, long after
the time of weeping, I could see
the blonde child, skipping
along the sand road; the radiance.

4

Running through the Heart of Storms
(Returning to Poland—Krakow, 2013)

It is your destiny to move your wand, / To wake up storms, to run through the heart of storms, / To lay bare a monument like a nest in the thickets, / Though all you wanted was to pluck a few roses, wrote Czeslaw Milosz, the Polish Nobel Laureate for literature, in his poem "Days of Generation"[1] after he had experienced the Nazi occupation of his homeland, worked in the underground resistance, and been a witness to the devastation of his country, Poland—and indeed all of Europe—in World War II.

~

It is May 2013, eighty years since the Nazi party with its brown shirts came into existence and began its ascent to power in 1933. My husband and I are traveling from Berlin where we have explored the city, where we could not shake the chill, like the May weather. The Nazi regime and the ensuing Communist one that, like the Wall which came down in November 1989, have left behind other indelible marks. Each of my three children were born in the years just before the wall between East and West Berlin came down in November 1989. Thereafter the iron curtain was lifted from the countries where my parents were born. This history pulls at me as if to say I (perhaps each of us in my family) need to claim a relationship to it.

---

1. Milosz, *The Collected Poems, 1931–1987*, 32.

And, as on the former trip in 2005, I notice again how the countryside, flat and green, the rain outside, reminds me of home, the Sumas Prairie, in the mighty Fraser River's Valley where my grandparents lived. The tiny houses, the old wood-sided barns, the country roads. Once more I travel to Poland; from Berlin the train takes us to the city of Katowice, in southern Poland, in what was the German province of Upper Silicia, and then on to Warsaw where we will change trains for Krakow.

On the train to Krakow a distinguished looking man in a suit introduces himself in English, after he hears my husband and me speaking. On his way home from a conference, he proffers his business card, a retired professor and a leading researcher in the field of telecommunications. He is pleased to offer recommendations of what to see while we're visiting Krakow. "It is worth a visit to the Salt Mines at Wieliska a short bus ride from the city," he says.

"The Schindler Factory near the Jewish Quarter is interesting," he continues, "though it's not the original enamel factory." He tells us how Steven Spielberg fictionalized some aspects of the story in the movie Schindler's list—the little girl in the red coat. In the movie, she is among the dead. In real life she is actually Roma Ligocka, he tells us. He means this metaphorically; she is an artist living in Germany and well-known in Poland.

The Girl in the Red Coat was published in Germany in 2002 and translated to English. Roma Ligocka is a cousin to Roman Polanski, who, as a young boy had been smuggled out of the ghetto—and when she saw the premier of *Schindler's List*, she understood at once the child depicted was *her*. Roma was born in Krakow in 1938, and so is one year older than my mother. Although she had been very young, memories dark and flickering from her earliest consciousness, from 1941 to 1943, stifled and hidden like the Jewish child she had been, appeared. Remembering her own small red coat, she began putting together the fragments of her past. From the images on screen, the traumatic memories of the early part of her life started to shift loose in the tremors of emotional trauma. In her transfixing memoir she has etched the voice of the Jewish child into the reader's imagination.

I have also been reading the twentieth-century Polish poet Anna Kamieńska, (1920–1986). During the Nazi occupation Kamieńska taught in underground schools. Of the bombardments during the war and of destruction, she writes that annihilation is preceded by a great light: "At first it fell from above, that beautiful, blinding, greenish light, so bright that it seemed to illuminate the earth's every wrinkle. That light illuminates every person, every cell, vein, artery like an x-ray; everything is ready for death. It irradiates and exposes all that is hidden most deeply—terror, the body's animal terror."[2] I am drawn to Kamieńska's poems with their themes of family, loss, grief. And I admire the honesty of her struggle with, or toward, religious faith, or what she might describe as the light of a life-giving source. "I don't believe in the other world. But I don't believe in this world either / if it's not penetrated by light" she writes in *Astonishments*.[3]

The Polish man on the train is about sixty and has lived his whole life in Krakow. He tells us there are very few Jews living in Krakow. He thinks perhaps two hundred would be a good estimate, a number that Ligocka also offers in her 2002 book. He surmises that the keepers of the Holocaust memorial at Auschwitz-Birkenau, close by, and those who work in kosher restaurants, bookstores, and so on, in Krakow's Jewish quarter, Kazimierz, are likely not Jewish.

"Kazimierz was nearly denuded of Jews already then, as it is most entirely denuded of them now," writes Eva Hoffman reflecting on her return trip to Krakow as a teenager, after immigrating to Canada as a young teen.[4] Hoffman, whose parents survived the Holocaust in hiding in Ukraine, was born in 1945 and lived in Krakow until age thirteen when her family immigrated to Vancouver, my home city. A professor of Literature at Yale, she has lived in New York and London. Her book, *After Such Knowledge*, explores the questions of what to remember, and how to remember, particularly in the case where the Holocaust has, for the most part, been considered within the context of World War II.

These are questions I have been pondering, given my heritage and my ancestral homeplace of Poland. Hoffman points out that after the war, the Holocaust was not a subject of public discussion. In Eastern Europe, this was because of censorship and political repression. "But in the West and other parts of the 'free world' as well, the early 1950s was a period of forgetfulness."[5] I think of the post-war injunction to "never forget" and of the exhortation to "remember" regarding the Holocaust, that I would learn about in junior high, in the seventies.

2. Kamieńska, *In That Great River*, 2.

3. Kamieńska, *Astonishments*, 43.

4. Hoffman, *After Such Knowledge*, 224.

5. Ibid., 84.

The next generation is not held responsible for the past, *but for the way it remembers the past*, said Elie Wiesel, a survivor of Auschwitz.[6]

Not being Jewish, I try to consider the nuances of each phrase. "Never forget"—a warning that conveys if we forget what happened, it is likely to happen again. Perhaps never forget is a collective act. "Remember" seems more intimate. Remember the individual, the *individual's* story.

"Are you going to Auschwitz?" the scientist asks. "It's a very sad place, but you should go."

The train is slowing. As we roll into the outskirts of Krakow, the scene is pastoral, the ploughed spring fields, the tidy farmyards and homes.

~

I had first seen the grainy images, projected by a stream of light onto a screen, the click-click-click of the reels, in my grade nine Social Studies class at the Mennonite high school I attended where German language classes were required. I was fourteen. In the first few moments of darkness, some of my classmates settled their heads into arm crooks on the desktop. But I sat upright, compelled into absorption by the grey smoking cities, marching soldiers, and the hollowed faces, skeletal bodies that followed.

Grainy images. Frame by frame. In black and white.

The German invasion of Poland. Operation Barbarossa in Ukraine. The Holocaust. My mother from Poland, my father from Ukraine, I understood *this* was also part of their past and here was I, in my grade nine Canadian classroom, watching these films, taking it all in.

The past was rarely talked about in our family. Even so, it presented itself in these particular ways: my grandparents' mother tongue, my parents' inflections of speech together with the absence of their stories, and a brother "killed in the war" on both my parents' sides. And of my parents' and grandparents' generation, "who have lived the worst of this century in European history," Patricia Hampl, in her book *A Romantic Education*, observes, "it's as if they are intent upon protecting the rest of us." She says we children born after the war aren't survivors in the literal sense, but because our parents are survivors, to them, we have in a symbolic sense been passed over.[7] Yet, those who lived through loss pass something of their experiences on in silent and ritualized ways. As a child, I understood that somehow,

6. Wiesel, *From the Kingdom of Memory*, 194.

7. Hampl, *A Romantic Education*, 181.

the marginalized past now had everything to do with the primacy of family, underscored by our many gatherings with my mother's family, from Christmas to Easter and all throughout the year.

~

The bright sky is cloudless, but the white horses are as drifting clouds leading their carriages through the Old Town of Krakow. The old world charm of cobblestone and outdoor cafés with red umbrellas is as expected in this tourist destination. Beyond the Old Town's walls and *Wawel* castle on the hill, the glistening river, lazy and serpentine, is compensating for the drab and grey apartments, the shabby districts of Krakow we walk through.

Beneath the bridge, the great Vistula is a silver cord that ties the present to the past.

Over the bridge lies the Jewish Quarter. Nearby is the Schindler's factory museum. It's just a random factory that houses a museum in an industrial district. The museum exhibit consists of photographs and quotes discussing the interwar period between World War I and II, Polish Independence, then the Nazi Occupation, and the deportations. Oskar Schindler, born in Czechoslovakia, was a Nazi intelligence officer who came to Krakow to run a factory under the *Reich*. While the museum is a testament to the shift in Schindler's moral view, as I proceed through the exhibits I sense in the Polish point of view, as it is printed on the placards, with respect to anti-Semitism and the Holocaust overall, that it was after all, perpetrated by the Germans. In the German Jewish conversation, as Eva Hoffmann states, one knows clearly who the victims were, and who the villains. She suggests that the ambiguities of Polish history make it a clearly contested past and "in the Polish Jewish transactions, a shared interpretation has yet to be achieved."[8]

Moreover, while I have quoted lines from Czeslaw Milosz, who is exceptional for his recognition of and reckoning with his own conscience, and by implication his Christian conscience, Hoffman contends in the early years following the war, even the most humane, creative, and compassionate responses did not yet perceive the Holocaust as separate from the war.[9]

8. Hoffman, *After Such Knowledge*, 142.
9. Ibid., 22.

Survivor Elie Wiesel has described the Holocaust as a unique event.[10] I see the importance of addressing it in its singularity. Conversely, as I address my family's experience in Poland, in writing about the war the idea of not addressing the Holocaust is a vexing one. If the stories are separate, they are horribly tangled.

Until 1989 there was no public discussion about the Holocaust in Poland, which of course might be a result of censorship under the Communist era that immediately followed.[11]

There are more recent books about the war and those in Poland who protected and concealed the presence of their Jewish neighbors, such as the *Zookeeper's Wife* by Diane Ackerman. This memoir tells the story of Jan and Antonina Zabinski, keepers of the Warsaw Zoo who hid their neighbors where the animals had lived. In 1968, *Yad Vashem* honored them, and others, as Righteous Among the Nations in a tree-planting ceremony on the hill of remembrance.

～

The sign on the highway says *Oswiecim* with a directional arrow. In German the town is called Auschwitz. The countryside reminds me of driving to the Mennonite settlement of Yarrow on the Sumas Prairie back home near my grandparents' farm.

When we decided to travel to Krakow, we came to the conclusion that a return to Poland would entail a visit to Auschwitz, and so I attempted to prepare myself ahead of time, and to allow for time and solitude, so as not to treat this as a sightseeing excursion. Instead of a tour bus, we planned to take the early morning train to Auschwitz. Somehow, I thought it would seem more historic, even fitting. I did not want to purchase a "tour" of the camp sold at the tourist kiosks in the Old Town. We were to set off early and arrive before the buses. We were to walk through on our own without a guide. I didn't know quite what to expect, although I had been to *Yad Vashem*, the memorial on the hillside in Israel, the strangeness of a train car, one that had transported Jews to death camps in Poland, placed on the hillside in Israel among the pines, in memoriam. I was not exactly looking forward to the day, but we had planned for it.

As we near the train station, an older man approaches us and tells us he can get us there faster than the train will. We have missed the direct train;

10. Wiesel, *From the Kingdom of Memory*, 174.
11. Hoffman, *After Such Knowledge*, 138.

the one we are trying to catch will make stops along the way. By the time we get there it will be crowded, he warns, and points to his car. This is how he makes an income. Merek is seventy-something with a wiry build. His lined, tanned face is contrasted by closely trimmed white hair. We climb into the back seat of his Mercedes sedan, a pack of Viceroys between the two front seats. We soon discover he is a chain-smoker,

This drive early in the morning couldn't be more beautiful. Green fields, villages with lovely homes, a castle on a hilltop in the distance. But reminders, too. An old spa hotel overlooking the valley we drive through was once Gestapo headquarters, Merek points out. The two-lane roadway is lined with trees, their filigreed shadows splashing the asphalt. Into a dense forest brightened by morning sun. Out again. Merek tailgates, as if to remind me this is not a leisurely drive in the country. We pass two men in a wooden cart led by a chestnut horse with a blonde mane.

He has just announced it is twenty more kilometers. He points out a coal mine, Kapanya, where prisoners from the camp worked. I see older people waiting along the roadside at a bus stop and realize they were children then.

As we near the town, there are railway tracks to our right. The same tracks once used for the transports. A Toyota sign, hotels, KFC, a billboard for "Life Festival—June 2013—Sting and Red Hot Chili Peppers," Planet Cinema, a mall. A painter's palette of bright tulips bloom beside the tracks.

Oswiecim's army garrison was taken over after the Polish army was defeated in 1939. At first it was a prison for Polish soldiers and political prisoners. Soon after, the sub-camps—the satellite camps—of Auschwitz were built.

There are coffee kiosks before the entrance. I am astonished by the number of buses.

I notice the school groups, the teenagers joking and jostling in line, talking as we walk through the entrance, under the banner of the iron gate: *Arbeit Macht Frei.*

Inside the gates, the grounds get busier. One student has his earbuds in, iPod slung around his neck and I can hear the muted tinny sound of rap music. As we proceed through the barracks, crammed into the rooms, our bodies, are pressed close together.

In one exhibit, the roomful of suitcases, I note handwritten names, addresses, and telephone numbers on them. These traces of their lives are palpable. I notice too those Jewish surnames in common with my own Germanic and Mennonite heritage—Isaac, Krause, Neumann . . .

It is an eerie sight, the line of people, single-file, entering the doorway of the crematorium.

We walk back out into the sunlight and blink. The birds are singing. A quiet breeze blows through the compound, traffic hums past on a freeway that runs beside.

By the time we exit the gates beneath the banner, each of us is silent.

~

A few kilometers away is Auschwitz II—Birkenau. The barracks were built from the materials of seven demolished villages: Brzezinka, Babice, Broszkowice, Rajsk, Plawy, Harmeze, and Brzeszcze-Budy. The name Birkenau was given because of the Birch trees.

There is one train car in memoriam of a people. Visitors place stones on it.

Primo Levi, a survivor of this place, wrote of the fields of green grass stretching out into an appalling vastness that here the ashes of a multitude were spread.[12]

I leave with questions swirling like the leaves in this afternoon gust of wind. Before we came to *Oswiecim* I had thought about what it might be like to live in the town whose name was given to the infamous death camp.
The town continues to grow despite (or because of?) these sites in its midst. Along the road that leads to Birkenau, there is a subdivision. Someone is building a new house.

~

In her meditation on the aftermath of the Holocaust, written sixty years after the war, Eva Hoffman reflects on the appropriate response. Can there be one? Can one be demanded? If there is no response, she writes,

---

12. Levi, *Auschwitz Report*, 75.

it cannot be asked for. However, if people respond by examining their prejudice, offering their acknowledgement, or even their apologies, she believes that people in her place—those who have experienced what I have not—must respond to gestures of good faith, "recognize the recognition." And still, the enormity of it all renders it impossible to truly comprehend. Profoundly, Hoffman says, "We cannot ask of others what we might not be able to do ourselves—or what is impossible to accomplish."[13]

At her following words I catch my breath, as when astonished by the light of dawn.

> Sixty years later, what was so horrifically and still puzzlingly done here cannot be undone. Sixty years later, I feel, this is the only thing that can be done to acknowledge, turn, bend towards the victims rather than away from them. There can be no other recompense, no other closure. Sixty years later, I think, and after all that can be done has been done it may also be time to turn away, gently, to let this go.[14]

Hoffman is the child of parents who emerged from hiding to discover they had lost everyone and everything they had known.

Simone Weil, philosopher, writer, and political activist, a Jew who converted to Christianity, held that true learning is seeing things as they really are. In her life and writing she took up the question that Christ posed— Who is your neighbor?—when he told the parable of the Good Samaritan. I believe it is no coincidence that Rembrandt's painting entitled *The Good Samaritan* hangs in Poland, in Krakow's Czartoryski Museum. Rembrandt, the Dutch master of the 1600s, whose work reveals Christian themes and who observed closely Amsterdam's Jewish population, comments by his art. It is timeless.

In my own heritage there has been a return to Poland by scholars, to revisit the sites of former Mennonite communities, reviving their historical religious context, but also to consider or reconsider their role in Poland and Russia prior to and under German occupation.

What was it like to have lived in Poland then? To have lived at this time? The memories of young children grown old, born in those rural

13. Hoffman, *After Such Knowledge*, 233.

14. Ibid., 233.

villages of Mennonites, somewhat insulated and insular, shed a slant of light for me today.

And, we, the children born after this time, are not only born into an elegy, but are charged to consider how the past affects us, its reverberations "like a silent bell" hearkening the future.

~

On this late afternoon day in May 2013, my husband and I return to Kazimierz, to the scene of previous deportations. The sun is still shining as we walk over the bridge. On the banks of the Vistula below, people are strolling, riding bikes, picnicking on blankets.

We sit down in an outdoor café to have a light dinner of potato *latkes* (My mother will later tell me as a young child in Poland potato pancakes were her favorite dish, which my grandmother occasionally made). As we eat, we listen to a girl sing a popular Jewish folk song in Hebrew, the music imbuing a mix of longing and belonging, a distinctiveness to this place that once was the center of Jewish life and culture in this historic city. The girl's melodic voice is thick and sweet as the Hebrew words of a flatted scale flow over the newly-laid cobblestones of the square. The acoustics are enhanced by the restored walls of the freshly plastered pink and yellow buildings surrounding us. Even though I know she is singing for tourists, in my own disarticulation, I savor the sound.

"Hava Nagila" was first a wordless song (*nigum*) from Eastern Europe, then brought to Palestine with the early Hasids. In 1905, to establish a national identity, a musician and Zionist set this song, among others, to the Hebrew language in order to create a national identity among the many diverse communities of Jews living in Jerusalem. Its few words are from Psalm 118:24. *This is the day that the Lord has made, let us rejoice and be glad in it.* As a Canadian child, I remember singing a simple song at my Mennonite Sunday school; these same words, this verse, but in C major, a cheerful chorus.

The evening clouds are a linen curtain drawn over the day. It is time to leave. I am a visitor here, and disquieted by silent and strong emotions.

Kanada

(the warehouses were so named because Canada was thought to
be a country of great riches)

>At the Entrance

a black and white photograph

shows a young boy, holding

two smaller boys by the hand,
one on each side. Behind him

walk women with babies.

Inside, behind glass,

roomfuls
of crutches, leg braces, prosthetic legs, silver

spoons, forks, pitchers, tin pots, bowls, even
packets of pepper,

shaving brushes, combs,

suitcases with names, house numbers,
the street, and city printed on,

children's shoes,
pumps, sandals, heels, leather
men's shoes,

baby clothes,

blank eye-
glasses,

and prayer shawls.

Unsayable things.

Hallways   and   hallways
                    lined
          with photographs,

a room full of *empty*

                    canisters
                              (zyclon B pellets turned to gas).

At the Exit>
                    a glass urn *filled*

                              with ash,

                                        so horribly clear.

Silence

5

Poland, 1930s

In the 1930s, the nation of Poland, in existence once more after disappearing and being absorbed by the Russian empire for more than a century, was a place with people of different ethnicities and nationalities. Among them, Ukrainians and Germans called Poland home.

~

While Poland was home to them, Mennonites, colonists, did not feel connected to the Polish State created after World War I and identified themselves as German.[1] From 1928 to 1934, German organizations and Polish political parties were active in trying to attract ethnic Germans, but by 1936 German organizations intensified under The Third Reich's program of unifying all Germans, including those that lived abroad.[2] Thus, the Polish government began to enforce repressions for those who were not Polish or did not identify as Polish. In areas of Ukrainian ethnicity, this entailed burning books, closing schools and institutions, enforcing censorship, and beating people. And, with respect to Dutch colonization in Poland which includes the Lutherans, Mennonites, and Catholics of the Vistula Delta, such colonists were now identified as "German" and were affected by repressions and "anti-German acts."[3]

1. Marchlewski, *Hollanders during World War II*, 2.
2. Ibid., 2.
3. Ibid., 3.

Moreover, Germany provided financial aid to German farmers in Poland when most people were losing their farms during the economic crisis that began in 1928. One point of interest pertaining to my mother's family is that her grandfather Kliewer's water-powered flour mill had been sold. However, at the point of payment the Polish government devalued the currency.

Also, because Poland was inhabited by Germans, various organizations supported by the German Ministry of Foreign Affairs sprang up in the late 1930s. Already in 1924, the right wing party the *Deutscher Volksverband* (German People's Union in Poland, or *DVV*), with its National Socialist ideology, was formed in central Poland and most active in Lodz.[4] By 1938, local structures of the *DVV* had formed.[5]

These circumstances were like dry tinder accumulating. The first strike of the match occurred on June 15, 1934, when the Polish Minister of Internal Affairs was assassinated by a Ukrainian. In response, the Polish dictator Jozef Pilsudksi created a prison for suspected subversives and political opponents of the regime in what was a former Tsarist prison and barracks. It was named *Bereza Kartuska*, which means "place of isolation." Czeslaw Milosz identified *Bereza Kartuska* as a concentration camp, as did Ukrainian sources, although in 2007 the Polish government successfully objected to the use of the term, identifying the prison as a "seclusion camp" instead. Later, and ironically, the Soviets would cite the existence of the prison as an indication that Poland's president was a fascist.[6]

By June 1937, the leaders of the larger German Mennonite community—the church leaders—would publish a statement saying the organizing structure of the Mennonite congregations (the German Mennonite Conference) would give up the principle of non-resistance. While some had let it go in the First World War, it was one of the core tenets of their Anabaptist forebears and founder Menno Simons, and a distinguishing trait up until this time.[7]

During this time, along with mounting financial instability, there was also a growing anti-Semitic climate in Poland. By October 1937, those

---

4. Wikipedia, *Deutscher Volksverband.*

5. Marchlewski, "Hollanders During World War II, and Their Post-War Situation" 3; Wikipedia, *Deutscher Volksverband.*

6. Wikipedia, *Bereza Kartuska Prison*; Milosz, *The History of Polish Literature*, 383.

7. Schroeder, "Mennonite Nazi Collaboration," 6.

identified as financial criminals were being sent to *Bereza Kartuska*. On March 24th, 1938, the *London Times* reported from Warsaw that "twelve speculators, mostly Jews, were sent today to the concentration camp at Bereza." The news article stated that these men were disseminating false information with a view to depreciating security prices and creating a financial panic. It reported that "many Jews were beaten when they tried to draw their savings from the bank," and that "anti-Semitism in Poland is growing, aggravated by the influx of Polish Jews driven out of other countries . . . Jews are now returning in large numbers from Austria . . . . "[8]

To more fully explore my own family story, I turn to old yellowed issues of a Mennonite publication called the *Mennontische Rundschau*. My Aunt Ella has saved them from among my grandfather's few papers. Here is a series of weekly articles in German, dated June to August 1968, entitled "Stories of the Mennonites and the Mennonite Brethren Church in Deutsch Wymyschle, Poland," by Robert Foth. Mr. Foth was a resident of the ancestral village before and during the 1930s, but actually wrote the information in 1949, which he later published in the newspaper in 1968. In the fifth *fortsetzung* (excerpt), dated July 5th, under the heading, "Die Verfolgung der Deutschen in Polen 1938–39," I read this writer's perspective on the events unfolding. "Up until the death of the leader, Jozef Pilsudski," in 1935 (of cancer) "it was good in Poland for Germans. After his death, it was very different."[9]

Pilsudski had been the first state leader of the newly independent Poland from 1918 to 1923, when he retired. Poland's first president of the Republic of Poland, Gabriel Narutowicz, had been assassinated one week after the election by a right-wing fanatic. In the civil unrest, mounting unemployment, and the economic crisis of these years, the new President, Stanislaw Wojciechowski, stepped down. Ignacy Moscicki would become president (from 1926 to 1939), and Pilsudski would return to politics to become, in effect, a dictator primarily concerned with military matters and foreign affairs. Pilsudski's foreign policy was to maintain good relationships with Germany and the Soviet Union.[10]

Foth writes that at this point in 1935, the rights of colonists began to shrink and the government soon tightened their grip on the unemployed,

8. *The Times* March 24, 1938. "Anti-Jewish Agitation in Poland."

9. Foth, "Geschichte der Mennoniten und MB," July 3, 1968.

10. Wikipedia, *Pilsudski*.

or those who were not nationals, and began to harass those who would not identify with Polish nationalism. The Polish media severely maligned those who identified as German.

It is possible that repressions may have been a reason the *DVV* attracted membership from those identified as German, even Mennonites, conservative as they were and separatist in their religious sense of not being "of the world." For some, over time, it seems the idea of national or ethnic identity appealed more strongly than religious Mennonite identity. Or as Wojciech Marchlewski, a Polish scholar interested in the Dutch ancestry of the Mennonites (who were originally called "Hollanders"), has expressed it, religious myth and national myth were combined. What I will learn in the years following my 2013 trip, is that North American and European scholars of Mennonite history have begun to explore how the idea of a Mennonite ethnic identity was built on and supported by the rise of Aryanism and National Socialism during the decade of the 1930s.[11] Mennonite self-identity as a community "set apart" became absorbed by the racialized concept of the German nation as a "separate people" or *Volk*.[12]

Focusing the lens for a moment on hindsight, when the question was asked why the Mennonites accepted Nazi Germany's policy of unification, a simple answer would be the economic crisis. When Hitler came to power, farmers didn't lose their farms.[13] But the consequences of identifying with the German language and culture, and rising Nazism, would prove to cast a dark heaviness over the Mennonites who had, for centuries, lived in Poland. It's also true that those Mennonites (pastors) who published critiques about supporting the policy of the German *Reich* were later sent to concentration camps, but those speaking out were the exception.[14]

The yellowed newspaper provides more insight. By 1938, due to the German *Ausland* propaganda, the sweeping rhetoric of Adolf Hitler, and the growth of his power and popularity in Germany, hatred of Germans was growing daily in Poland. The Polish police began random searches of German homes. They searched for letters, newspapers, both from inside and outside of Poland. Germans were beaten. "You didn't dare go into the

11. Huber, "Historians Address Nazi Influence on Mennonites at Mennonite World Conference Assembly," para. 2.

12. Roth, "Historians Confront hard truths of Nazi era," para. 11.

13. Marchlewski, "Hollanders During World War II, and Their Post-War Situation," 2.

14. Ibid., 2.

street. What could the Mennonites living outside of the borders of Germany do? We were not political. And flight out of Poland was unlikely," writes Foth.

Henry, my mother's older brother, was almost twelve years old at that time. When I asked him what it was like for them as Germans, he said, "My dad had a good relationship with his Polish neighbors. It was peaceful in the village and surroundings, but dangerous in unfamiliar areas or larger towns. Our dad spoke fluent Polish when he went to another town for supplies."

When I think of my grandfather, the image that comes to mind is of him with his neighbor, Mr. Schmidt, also an immigrant from Poland to Canada, sitting at the front of my grandparents' house in our hometown, side by side on a wooden bench, chatting. Or sometimes in the softer lawn chairs unfolded for longer visits to pass an afternoon. It's easy to imagine him chatting on the streets of Gabin, the nearest larger town to Wymyschle. A kind of conversation that begins with the salutary, "How goes it?" then the long pauses of an amiable exchange, "Ah, it goes," as the men look out over the street and agree to themselves, "Mmh, hmm. Beautiful day. Mmh, hmm." In Poland the two men would have smoked tobacco. In his later years in Canada, my grandfather would have offered the neighbor a peppermint.

The date states March 1st, 1939: Wymyschle, Poland. I am looking at a copy of a letter written by my mother's brother, fifteen-year-old David, to his cousin Ernst, a boy his own age who lived in Acme, Alberta and whose world was very different from David's Poland. I notice how the fine cursive writing of David's hand runs straight across the unlined page (Had he taken the time to place a ruled page beneath the blank one?). David's voice in first-person present tense flows from the fountain pen. Inquisitive and polite. My mother and aunts have said their oldest brother was gentle-natured; always patient.

David's mother (my grandmother) and Ernst's mother were half-sisters. Mathilde was the daughter of their father Kornelius Kliewer's second marriage to his deceased wife's sister. So the women were not only half-sisters, they were also cousins. But this would not have been unusual in a time when marriages were for convenience, concerned with keeping property within the family, or with finding immediate help for a widower with five children to raise (and five more children to be born.) The half-sister Mathilde and her husband had had four sons in Poland, but each one had died in childhood. With only one son, their youngest Ernst, they decided to move to Canada in the late 1920s. At that time, my grandparents remained behind because the older couple who had taken in my grandmother at three days old, following her mother's death, were not accepted by Canadian immigration. Specifically, Paulina, *Babtjche*, had trachoma.

At the time of the letter, David no longer goes to school. He has completed his formal education after finishing the third *Abteilung* (section). He writes that younger brother Heinrich is repeating the third and final section for the third time (which my uncle Henry, in his eighties, and financially successful, jokes about today.) Johann is in his first year, the last section, and their sister Martha is in her first year of school. In school the children learn Polish and German. David now lives with his (and Ernst's) maternal grandparents, known as " the miller" Kliewers, in a fine red brick house about a mile down the village road from his parents' home. Because his grandparents no longer have a hired housemaid, David helps his grandmother with chores and milking the cows. It has been a cold winter; David mentions skating on the nearby pond. He tells Ernst that he has three brothers and four sisters: Heinrich, Johann, Wilhelm, Martha, Anna, and Emilie; the youngest, at two weeks old, does not yet have a name. (This is my mother, born on February 18th, 1939. Her name will be Erna). *Babtjche*, who lives with them, helps mother with cooking, cleaning, and washing.

This is David's simple life in a rural Mennonite village in Poland, in early 1939.

On Friday, September 1st, 1939, the German army entered Poland by sea near Danzig where about 80 percent of its population was German. It had been a free city under the League of Nations since 1918 following World War I. Hitler wanted access to the sea from East Prussia, a thin corridor of land through Poland from the Baltic to East Prussia. On a small peninsula near Danzig, where the Vistula pours out into the Baltic Sea, the first German shot was fired.

In 1939, Mennonite newspapers published articles that viewed the German occupation as breaking the last border that separated the nation (of the *Volksdeutsche*), "in the name of God."[15]

15. Marchlewski, "Hollanders During World War II, and Their Post-War Situation," 2.

I borrow the following account which adds further context. It comes from the personal family history of Eric L. Ratzlaff, a former Wymyschle resident married to my grandfather's sister. "Early in the morning on Friday, September 1, 1939, I put the ear phones of my little transistor radio on and heard the speech of the Polish President, Ignacy Moscicki, who stated, "The archenemy of Poland wants a piece of our garment but we will give them none, not even a button will they get. We will fight till victory or death."[16]

The old yellowed newspaper reveals, according to Mr. Foth, that in the small community of Wymyschle, from August 24 to 26, 1939, six young men were called up to the Polish army. Names are not provided, so I don't know if they were Mennonite. There were also a few Lutheran and Polish residents in the village, perhaps married into Mennonite families.

~

In the first days of the September campaign, the Polish police began mass arrests of Germans. Accounts of killings of Germans in Poland leading up to and during the first weeks of the German invasion have recently been the focus of both Polish and German historians, although the information is in dispute as German accounts were recorded during the war by the German *Abwehr* (military), and Polish accounts have been influenced by communist historiography.

Rumors of saboteurs and spies were rampant and "spy hysteria" set in. Many ethnic German people were robbed or lynched. In the area of Kazun, not far from my mother's village, but close to the area of the Modlin Fortress across the river, an area in the path of the Germans' 5th column—and perhaps why Germans living there were accused of spying and sabotage—events were particularly dramatic. The castle had been bombed. In the Mennonite congregation of Deutsch Kazun, one of the elders was arrested and executed in front of other members of the congregation, probably by soldiers or police. Other members of the congregation were arrested by Polish police, never heard from again. Seventeen more members of the Deutsch Kazun church would be killed during military actions, and all boys and men between age seventeen and sixty would be arrested. Also in neighboring Gabin, an Evangelical pastor was executed. He had been

---

16. Ratzlaff, *From the Don to the Fraser*, 36.

a leader of a local unit of the *Deutscher Volksverband*. He was accused of sabotage, but without a trial, so it's not known if it was true.[17]

Additionally, Foth's recounting states that after the outbreak of war, fourteen or fifteen men were arrested from the family village, along with many other Germans from the surrounding area and villages. Foth says no one knew why, or if they would ever see them again. They were taken from the village by truck. My uncle Henry tells me more particularly that, in Wymyschle, my grandfather, Wilhelm, age thirty-nine, was arrested together with his half-brother Erhard.

Eric Ratzlaff, who I have previously quoted, writes in his personal account of this time that he hid in a hayloft for two days. This is what he remembered:

> On September 2nd, my two brothers-in-law, Erhard Ratzlaff and Wilhelm Schroeder, had to come to Gombin[18] to the police station "for interrogation" (his quotation marks). Since they did not return, my wife asked me to go to Gombin to find out what happened to them. I went to Gombin, put my bicycle into a store whose owner knew me, and went to the police station. I was received by the chief of police whom I knew personally. He looked at me and at my identification papers and said hastily, "Go Home! You will not be interrogated." I took his advice and went to the Catholic priest in Czermno, Dr. Helenowski, to find out what this was all about. When the priest called the police in Gombin to find out why they were kept there, he got the reply that they were in "protective custody" (again, his quotation marks) and would be interned for the rest of the war.
>
> Now I knew it all: Erhard and Wilhelm were members of the Volksverband, a German political organization who stood up for the rights of Germans in Poland, [he concludes].

I wonder if this is fact or conjecture, because in historical data about the Mennonites here, these two men are not listed as members. I do, however, discover that one individual with the same name, "Erich Raztlaff," (different or incorrect spelling) and three other Mennonite men from the broader region were registered members of the *Volksverband* since 1938.[19]

---

17. Marchlewski, "Hollanders During World War II, and Their Post-War Situation," 3. See also Schroeder Thiessen and Showalter, *A Life Displaced*, 9.

18. Ratzlaff uses the German name of Gabin.

19. Marchlewski, "Hollanders During World War II, and Their Post-War Situation," 3.

In the old newspaper, Foth goes on to say that on September 4th, 1939, twenty-six other German men from the area were taken: "I was one of them." Taken in chains on a truck to Gostynin, a town nearby, fortunate, he says, not to be beaten along the way. In Gostynin, there was a much larger group of Germans, "and from there, 159 of us were taken by train to Warsaw. Of this group we went no further—the German army intercepted and freed us on September 9th at the Leanov Station." How frightening the experience was, he states, how violent, and how those four days had seemed like four weeks.

"We were in constant threat of being shot when the train stopped. If the two Polish officers had not protected us we would have been killed," he conjectures, possibly by the Polish refugees fleeing the Germans. The other threat came from the German airplanes circling the trains, who could have bombed them at any moment.

He continues. Another six men were arrested on September 7th. These men went by foot, beaten severely along the way. When they neared Lodz, the men joined another larger transport of Germans. This group was freed by the German army there on September 9th.

What I now know about my grandfather and his half-brother, Erhard, is they were sent to Bereza Kartuska.

Statistics, both official and unofficial (which are more than twice as high), record the deaths. But testimonies from inmates reveal death through murder and torture during questioning.[20]

Yurij Luhovy, a Ukrainian Canadian filmmaker from Montreal whose father was in the camp, has made documentaries about the persecution of Ukrainians which includes information about the prison. He states that by September 1939 there were between 5,000 and 8,000 people held, up to seventy men in one room, some sleeping outside under the elements. When asked how his father got out, he answered, "[i]ronically it was because of the beginning of World War II and another occupation of Ukraine. In 1939, the Germans attacked Poland. The Nazis and the Red Army met in Brest Litovsk" (now in Belarus).[21]

---

20. Wikipedia, *Bereza Kartuska*.

21. Ponomarenko, "Yurij Luhovy on the Making of a Film about Bereza Kartuzka," para. 48.

According to his father's testimony, Luhovy says when the Poles in Bereza saw the Germans were advancing, all the police guards fled the camp at night. On September 18th, 1939, the local people opened the gates and released the prisoners. My uncle told me, perhaps according to my grandfather, the prison guards opened the gates themselves as they fled, and, Henry adds, that on September 17th, the Russians entered Poland from the east.[22]

Among the prisoners, my grandfather and his step-brother walked, or rather limped through open gates.

What I have come to learn about my grandfather is the wound in his leg, the physical wound that continued to seep, was not the result of a bullet from the war, as I imagined when I was a child. I later thought it might have been the result of a beating from angered Polish citizens after Germany's capitulation. But my mother tells me now it was inflicted by jackbooted guards in Bereza Kartuska who had kicked him repeatedly. A literal scar remained that never fully healed because my grandfather had diabetes.

My mother remembers when they were already living in Canada, his leg wound festered when he worked in the fields in summers, that he was once bed-ridden after he had worked in the heat of the raspberry rows on the farm on the Sumas prairie, his pant leg rubbing against the sore. As I think of it, he walked slowly, with a slight limp, but when I was young it seemed simply to be the way he walked, the gait of an old man, my Opa, with his heavy belly and his sugar diabetes. I can still envision my grandmother wrapping my grandfather's leg in gauze, the chipped white enamel bowl of warm water for washing it, the blueness of his foot.

Mr. Foth concludes his 1968 newspaper account of the weeks in August and September 1939 by stating that of those taken and those who came back, many were lame or bore the marks of beatings. "We thought they would recuperate, but it was obvious that many suffered badly. In spite of this, we were fortunate compared to others."

He goes on to write about the discovery of mass graves of Germans in the vicinity of Warsaw. This discovery became well-known and thousands went to find their loved ones, he notes. "Those from a neighboring Evangelical German congregation, eighty men, were found, and with them, another thirty from other churches. They were then buried individually."

22. Marchlewski also states that when the prison guards fled they opened the gates.

The sound of grief is difficult to express," he discloses all those years later. "I can't describe it. Had these unfortunate people only been shot, perhaps the people's grief would not be so difficult as now. But it was clear they had been tortured."

As my father helps me transcribe the account, my mother says, "I remember those stories as a young child." I suspect she overheard them as the men gathered to speak, in low and hoarse tones.

I don't want to transcribe what Robert Foth has graphically written, but who will see and speak about war's brutality when eyes and tongues have been cut out?

The Prisoner

Bereza Kartuska
Polsie Province, Poland, 1939, (now Belarus)

> *"This body so frail and woundable /*
> *Which will remain when words fail us."*
>
> —Czeslaw Milosz

i.
The Place of Isolation is its name in full.
To prevent escape, it was encircled
by five lines of barbed wire, a moat, and finally,
high-voltage wire. Only the prisoner's last breath passed
through the barrier successfully.

A few grams of moldy bread, a can of thin coffee
or broth from rotten vegetables, just enough rations
to keep from starving. And torture,
wooden boards on the prisoner's back

struck by hammer blows.

Guards hosed down the cement so no one
might sit or lie down—bodies confined
to cells meant for fifteen, swelling to seventy,
then higher in the tide of a Second War.

ii.
And why him? —
tilling the river's soil,
a Mennonite farmer, whose ancestors
had settled the Vistula centuries before.

Why not him, too? The world's descent
began with a pact between dictators. It was the year

my mother was born, a baby that harvest,
when there came a knock at the door,

her father and uncle arrested, hands bound, feet
hobbled in chains, as other men
scurried to haystacks.
Someone passed on the word—a sentence
without trial.

iii.
He would have been shot, but the guards
fled as the Germans advanced and the Russians
closed in. Soldiers opened the gates.

iv.
Unnoticed as if a pickpocket child,
my mother snatched words
she lately remembers he said
long ago, talking with uncles,

chained to his brother
never before had he prayed
so hard to God as then, daily
their captors threatening execution.

When he returned to the village, the preacher
sagely spoke to him, let go of this and live
among your neighbors without bitterness.

v.
Perhaps that's why he scarcely spoke of it,
except to mention its name, an old man
in a new country when he later penned
his own brief obituary.

Besides the body,
what could capture the pain of those days,

or all he would come to endure

6

Gathered Fragments

1939–1943

The invasion of Poland by Germany, September 1st 1939, set off World War II. The fighting was most intense in the first weeks. In my mother's family, those weeks have been referred to as "the war in our area."

On the 17th of September, when Soviet forces crossed the Polish border from the east, the Polish president, Ignacy Moscicki, together with the entire government, fled to Romania where he would be interned as the result of pressure from Germany.

Memory is the other side of history.

On the night of the 17th and on the 18th of September, the Polish Cavalry came through Wymyschle. My aunt Annie (Anna) remembers how the soldiers walked by the barn where she, and perhaps the rest of the family stood, out of sight, in case something might happen. *Babtjche* was there in the barn, too, Anna recalls. While she sharply remembers the sabers of the Polish soldiers marching past the barn, her memory of this night, at age six or seven, is otherwise blunted by a child's fear, and, somewhat, by the passage of time.

And memory is not chronological, although fragments of it can be sorted, like pieces of a puzzle, its odd shape fitting into just the right place. I collect what remains of memory, along with the fragments, written in

1970 by a relative, that have also relied on memory. Events viewed from different angles. Remembered a little differently, although the truth of the experience is perfectly clear.

Today Anna also remembers that before the soldiers came through, Polish refugees had passed through their village. "They stayed with us," she says. Uncle Henry, too, recalls that refugees were sheltered in their house and in the barn.

One night, a paramilitary group passed through the village. There's a story recorded by the relative, Eric L. Ratzlaff, wherein the unofficial soldier in charge asked a Mennonite farmer if there were any Germans in the village. The farmer replied that these people were Dutch, and offered the group fruit from his plum trees and a place to camp. The farmer later speculated he may have prevented a massacre.

Henry recalls twelve German soldiers on horseback riding through the village, telling people the army was coming. A skirmish must have occurred because he remembers that Polish soldiers had been killed, as well as some horses the Germans had been riding. The German soldiers took horses from the farmers before they rode onward.

The battlefield drew closer.

Monday, September 18th, the first German soldiers entered the village according to family memory. I noted a slight discrepancy as I read from the Polish source I have been referring to, who points out that "the German army entered Kazun September 17, 1939, and on the same day seized Secymin, Wymsle, and Gabin."[1] The German military was strict to prevent scavenging or looting; reports were that another German farmer who had picked up some rounds of ammunition for a rifle was shot on the spot by a German officer. If not for this event, Deutsch Wymyschle was unscathed by the fighting. However, two kilometers away in Wymysle Polski, bombs called "block busters" were placed at a road crossing. When they blew up, they left deep craters where houses had been. And Gabin had been the target of raids from German *stukas* (bombers).

Long-married to my aunt Annie (Anna), uncle Gus—Gustav—a boy also born in Wymyschle but whose family moved to Gabin—remembers, when I spoke to him about that time, playing outside with his friends on the day the German planes flew overhead. Boys playing soldiers with sticks pointed their sticks at the planes in the sky until his father ran out,

---

1. Marchlewski, "Hollanders During World War II, and Their Post-War Situation," 4.

and shouted, "Get into the cellar!" At the time, "The Polish army was still marching," Uncle Gus said.

When the remnants of the Polish Northwestern Army surrendered, there were columns of POWs marching on the highway toward Gabin, and from there, on to POW camps.

Between 1939 and 1941, the occupational forces began deportations of Poles and throughout Poland and their farms were handed over to other ethnic Germans, over half a million. They came from other territories—the Soviet territories and the Baltic States—as part of "*Heim in Reich.*" (meaning "Home into the Empire") Many came to the nearby farming region of Gostynin.

As well, repressions were aimed at all those in the Polish resistance who had participated in arrests and execution of Germans.[2]

Here, however, "in the area of Gabin were also *Volksdeutsche* who secretly helped the Poles and even supported the activity of the resistance."[3] Reinhold Wegert—who I would later learn was then, and remained, my grandfather's friend—was one of the *Volksdeutsche* who supported the activity of the Polish underground. Other inhabitants of Wymyschle, such as Erich Ratzlaff,[4] spoke up to the Germans in defense of the Catholic rector of the Czermno parish, Father Helenowski.[5]

~

Of that day, September 18th, 1939, Eric L. Ratzlaff writes that the German army also entered nearby Gabin. The first order of business was the arrest and deportation of all political and social leaders. The *SS* came prepared with lists of leaders, Polish and Jewish, and also Catholic priests and Jewish rabbis. Protesting the beating of those arrested, Ratzlaff asked for the release of the Catholic Priest, Father Helenowski, and a Polish baker, Marjan Rojewski, who had come to his rescue many times when he, considered German, was in danger from Polish mobs. The baker was released; but not the priest. The priest was sent along with others to Oranienburg,

2. Ibid., 4.

3. Ibid., 10.

4. Ibid., 3. Marchlewski's spelling is Erich. He refers to Eric L. Ratzlaff and cites Ratzlaff's book.

5. Ibid., 6.

north of Berlin. It was one of the first detention facilities set up by the Nazis when they gained power in 1933, referred to as a concentration camp.

Ratzlaff writes in his self-published memoir, "One of the most unpleasant experiences was the treatment of the Jews by the Nazis."

On September 21st, an order came for all Jewish men of Gabin to assemble in the market square. On that day, the centuries-old synagogue built of wood, was doused with gasoline and set on fire.

This synagogue had stood in Gabin since 1710, and in it, a carved ark of oak that held the Torah scrolls. A legend had it that the ark was carved with only a single carving knife. The beautiful ornamental ark and an old brass chandelier that hailed from before the time of the first partition of Poland in 1772 were burnt. The fire spread to surrounding buildings, and the Torah scrolls and silver Torah ornaments that had been hidden in them were also lost.[6]

Under orders from the German military, the Jews were forced to register and to refill defense trenches. By October 1939, they were ordered to wear a yellow star on their clothes. The Germans reorganized the Polish civil administration.

The town was turned over to civil administration by the Germans, and as ordered, Jews organized the council of six elders (*Judenrat*). The *Judenrat* supplied workers each day for the clean-up of the town after the bombing raids.

The stories of people who share place and history are entangled. There is a detail that Mr. Ratzlaff has written in his memoir that illustrates this.

Ratzlaff became the liaison to the German authorities. The lead elder of the Jewish council was Moshe Wand (named also in the documents about Gabin published by Yad Vashem). When the *NSDAP* (*Nationalsozialistische Deutsche Arbeiterpartei*), or Nazi Party, arrived, the leader demanded carpets from Warsaw for his office. "Travel was restricted for Jews, so they sent Mojsze Wand to me to get a permit from me to travel to Warsaw," Ratzlaff writes. He goes on to say he knew this was illegal, but the mayor of the town insisted, and so Wand received the permit to travel to Warsaw. On his way back with the carpets, Wand was stopped, interrogated, and the carpets

---

6. Huberband, *Kiddush Hasem*, 305-07. Information is also from Ratzlaff, *From the Don to the Fraser*, 40.

confiscated. A bureaucratic investigation took place. The mayor of Gabin, along with the *Kreisleiter,* were each replaced by someone else. Ratzlaff would be assigned a teaching position in a school in Sierokowek, a former Polish village resettled by ethnic Germans relocated from Volhynia—an area that is in present-day Ukraine—as part of the mass population transfers of the Third Reich.

At the beginning of 1940, the Jews were "resettled" into a few streets in the northwest corner of the town. At first they were free to move about.

Then barbed wire was put around it.[7]

1939 to 1945—Jewish writer, Eva Hoffman, has called this period the silent years.

In my family history, for ethnic Germans, Mennonites, from Danzig and the Vistula delta, living in Ukraine (my father's family) and Poland (my mother's), these years were viewed as liberation from oppression and repression.

A Mennonite man from my mother's village (the man whose house the Polish woman resided in when we came to the village in 2005) was appointed interim mayor of Gabin after the Polish mayor was arrested. But the new position proved temporary. He was suspect, not anti-Polish enough, and replaced by an officer of the *Reich* from Germany. Nevertheless, opportunities were presented to the young adults from villages like Wymyschle. They moved to Gabin to take up jobs or open new business— positions and places left vacant by the local Polish and Jewish merchants.

When I later ask my mother what the adults thought about the oc- cupation, she says that though she did not know how her parents felt politi- cally, she understood many in the village did not view German occupation as "good" but that it was "better." This is the view of a very young child; tinged with hindsight? As far as the village children knew, "It was peaceful after the initial fighting in our area although the people noticed when the peddlers from Gabin stopped coming."

7. Ratzlaff, *From the Don to the Fraser,* 40. See also Wein, *Encyclopedia of Jewish Com- munities in Poland,* 154-56.

It was customary in those days for the Jewish travelling merchants from Gabin to come through the villages to sell their wares, produce, and dry goods. These people made their living from peddling and artisanal work. In the town of Gabin, in the shops, there had also been tailors, needle-workers, seamstresses and embroiderers, shoemakers, locksmiths, tinsmiths, furniture makers, barbers, bakers, and butchers.

Young sweethearts from Wymyschle married. Pictures of families from the village during this time reveal handsome young Mennonite men in their new and pressed German *Wehrmacht*—the German army—uniforms beside their wholesome-looking brides. "And then conscription was made mandatory and all the young men had to go," my mother reflects.

The *Wehrmacht* represented a division in conscience for the villagers between the army and the Nazi party, between a country's standing army and its political leadership. Shortly after the photographs were taken, these fellows were sent to battlefields, captured in Russia, and never heard from again; killed on the front or captured and sent to die in the Gulag. Some returned and rarely spoke about it.

⌒

During the early war years within my mother's village, within her family, life unfolded in the rhythm of the soil—planting, growing. Another baby girl (Ella) was born in 1940. My grandfather, at age forty, farmed his few acres; the crops would have been requisitioned by the German army. The other younger husbands and old-enough sons were sent to the Russian front. David was conscripted to the army in 1941 along with seventy-seven males from the village.

I think about some of the men in the village who, leading the church choir, or church youth group, taking on administrative positions under occupational forces in 1939, had donned uniforms when mandatory conscription took effect and were sent to the eastern front. My grandfather remained a civilian. I often think about the wound in his leg, whether it was from those kicks from hobnailed boots in the infamous Polish prison, Bereza Kartuska, and wonder if that was some sort of luck or providence.

⌒

In Gabin, by 1941, the first group of Jews was sent to Konin, to forced labor.

Ratzlaff writes that later that summer, there was a round-up into the square of all Jews, where they were kept for three days without food and water before they were loaded onto trucks and transported to Chelmno (named Kulm under the German occupation).

Sources from Yad Vashem, the memorial to the victims of the Holocaust in Jerusalem, state that the date of the liquidation of the Gombin ghetto was May 12th, 1942.[8]

~

In 1942 another baby girl, Mathilda (Tilly) was born.

My mother was almost three.

I think about the train ride toward Warsaw with my mother in August 2005 when she is telling me of finding out, perhaps overhearing her parents say, that the tailor and his wife were gone; about the memory of the matching maroon coats he had sewn for Erna and Emilie.

Another of my mother's memories is from when she was four in 1943, when David arrived home from the eastern front that June to heal. David had been in Stalingrad. He had not changed his clothes for three months when he arrived home, lice infested, and limping. Their mother washed and pressed his uniform for him. She cleaned and dressed his wound. She gathered the children for photographs before his furlough was over and he left once more.

Later that autumn—the sound of her mother's grief when the notice of death arrived by messenger.

I think of how a young child's memory clinging to a particular detail can be the truest moment. How a few words of the barest details contain within them the paradox of language, the sum of what, in the wake of that moment, the survivors and refugees didn't, or couldn't, talk about.

8. Wein, *Encyclopedia of Jewish Communities in Poland*, 154-56.

The Older Brother

in memory of David
November 16, 1924—October 24, 1943

Like apples from a crate, there were so many children
spilling out of the old farmhouse, its thick planks cut from pines,
older than I am now, more than eighty years. Casting a shade,

the pine-forest bordered one side of our village, and the stream
ran clear where we splashed, fresh and sparkling,
in the heat of summer. Between fields of barley

and farmyards, the white sandy path
cut a straight line, a dusty seam, now,
between present and past.

I pull memory like a loose thread, but carefully,
because I am afraid it could break.
You were sixteen when you were called up.

After that, my memory is a cloudy eye.
Not tall enough to be taken, I was too short
to have known. But remember when we
were small boys, you and me,
sent to play with the pigeons
roosting under the eaves when another baby was born?

Our childhood was simple—and vague—
before war. Why does only the sorrow grow
more vivid when I try to look back? In sepia,
the last photographs with you are from '43,
a boy-soldier without rank, on leave.
You survived Stalingrad. With a bullet wound,

your uniform infested with lice,
you limped home and after she cleaned you up,

our mother spent a few *zloty*

to pay a photographer. There's you, smiling,
squinting into the sun. With ribbons
in her braids, our sparrow-legged sister
perches on the handle-bars of your bicycle—
a stranger to her, have you coaxed her to smile?
You won't let her fall.

In another with Mother, are nine of us children, a nursery-
rhyme moment in war as the sunflowers bloom
beyond the split rail-fence.

And the last one, we little brothers in our suits
of short pants, you in your uniform, mended
and pressed. At the center,
you stand a head taller.

While you were with us, you didn't speak to me
of what you endured, or had seen. Born with a bad eye,
I couldn't see clearly. Your order to report for duty came

too soon. Later, the neighbor told me what you had said:
I won't be coming back.

As for the rest of us, we are children grown old.
Behind thick lenses I see you, the boy that you were,

my older brother, always, only nineteen.

Telegram, 1943

On the day the world ends, a bee circles a clover.
—Czeslaw Milosz

i.
The land's longest river carves a fertile valley
where hamlets grow fields of blonde wheat,
barley, and golden rapeseed. Coronas of sunflowers
face the sun. Yellow, too, are the fields of yarrow,

their flowers, according to myth, are known
to stop the bleeding wounds of soldiers.

And the river nourishes the acacias, their roots
fingering into the soil, and those of the pines, trunks
thickened by time, casting shadows long
after the bones of frolicking children have grown ethereal.

ii.
Fog had lifted early from the river.
Sun climbed into its seat on the cumulus clouds
to oversee the comings and goings of the village.
The dark earth had been dug,

the potatoes, with their many eyes,
already gathered and stored
under the house, in the darkness,
along with the onions.

Their sweetness
would cause you to weep.

The floor planks swept bare, the children
by now, were outside in the yard collecting
speckled eggs from the coop.

The echo of young laughter rang out,
perhaps at the cockerel strutting about.

But one and all stopped
at the ascent of her wail.

From her hands fell the note,
its official signature, a crashing weight,

the date stamped weeks before,
rifting now the ground she had known.

iii.
Whose memory can recall the messenger?
And was it then, that from the roof of the barn
the stork took flight? And could it have been
a black stork that year, the rare kind
that doesn't return after winter?

As if in a photograph, the particular is frozen.
The children will not forget how every hue
drained from that moment. Nor the thundering
silence that followed, through time suspended,

like the bee bumbling outside the hive
on that day, its faint humming in the yard
while the rest of the colony was prepared
for the coming of winter. On the chilled air

there hung the dim resonance of dying.

iv.
The black current is swift.
It cuts a swath through the land, where on one bank
roam the living, on the other, lie the dead,

and a mother must somehow learn to go on,

each foot in a disparate world.

7

Gathered Fragments

1944–1948

For everything there is a season,
and a time for every matter under heaven:
a time to be born, and a time to die;

—*Ecclesiastes 3:1–2a KJV*

In Poland, in my mother's family in 1944, the youngest and twelfth child, Bernhard (Bernie), was born. In 1944, old *Babtjche* died. These events of 1944 bring to my mind the third chapter of Ecclesiastes.

The meaning of the word *ecclesiastes* is translated as "gatherer"—one who gathers the people—and its writing considered to be one of the most powerful expressions of human life on this earth. If this book in Scripture on "a time for everything" was referring to the years from 1944 to 1948 in Europe, in Poland, its lament of *uprooting, killing, tearing down, weeping, mourning,* and *scattering stones* is most apt. Their antonyms, *healing, building, laughing, dancing,* and *gathering* could only be more fully considered much later, in the last years of a long life. According to tradition, Solomon wrote Ecclesiastes in his old age, having seen the worst of humanity alongside the good.

In 1944 my mother enters kindergarten: age five, her arm in front in compulsory salute at the start of each school day. This will be her first and last year in school.

In 1944, the remaining boys and men are ordered to report to the *Volksturm*, a rag-tag last resort to build up a German fighting force, made up of the too young and too old, without uniforms, just civilian clothes with a cloth armband, the word *Volksturm* on it. Henry, seventeen, now the oldest brother after David, is ordered to report. But short for his age, poor vision in one eye, and feigning a limp, he avoids conscription. Three times he is called up. Three times he limps to report to the officer behind a desk, three times declined, and each time once he's out of the officer's line of sight, how he runs!

By January 1945, it was clear that Germany was losing the war. In the Polish village there wasn't one family spared the losses. One Lutheran family lost four boys. The neighbors, another Kliewer family, lost three sons.

In western Poland, the Soviet troops were advancing. The fear of Stalinist repression and retribution was paramount.

The village mayor of Wymyschle received orders to evacuate. Some families, those who had possessions such as jewelry, or money for situations that might arise along the way, left immediately. My mother remembers that the family butchered meat, perhaps chickens or a pig, for their evacuation journey.

My mother's family left in a second, later group. The villagers loaded up their wagons and hitched them to horses. My mother, then five years old, almost six, remembers the weather on the day they left. "It was a cold sunny day."

My grandfather has written down, in his final years, that the family left their home on January 18th, 1945. Before leaving, my grandfather had to re-shoe the horses. This meant delay. The main roads were congested and clogged with columns of German soldiers, and the refugees were relegated to side roads causing further delays. Those who left earlier would make it out of Poland. And, as the story goes, the fate of the family was a matter of a fork in the road. Those from their group who turned right would make it, those who took the other road, my mother's family among them, would not.

²ᵇ *a time to plant, and a time to pluck up what is planted;*

My mother recalls the shooting and bombing along the way, but she doesn't remember that they were in the middle of a battlefield, taking cover from bullets in a snow-filled ditch until nightfall when the tanks were gone and the shooting grew quiet. The older children and adults remember this.

With horses and wagons they traveled almost as far as Thorn (Torun),[1] the medieval walled city on the banks of the Vistula, in the district of Danzig (Gdansk), and birthplace of Copernicus. There, the Red Army front lines caught up with them. *Zu dem Ort Leipe, vor Thorn*, my grandfather had written down twenty years later, in 1965. Leipe is the German name for the town of Lipno. Here at this place, about forty kilometers south of Torun, my grandparents and family were turned back by Russian soldiers, ordered to give over their horses and wagons.

The dread of the women and teenage girls when it came to the Soviet soldiers, the humiliation of the men are not mentioned.

Turned back, the refugees were stripped of whatever possessions they had left each time the group walked through a Polish village. In one, they were forced to disrobe, their clothes exchanged for torn and threadbare ones ("rags"). My Aunt Annie, who was ten at the time, reminds me that the people who took their clothing didn't have much either. "I still had a coat, so in one place, a woman took my coat from me because her daughter had none. On the way back, in another village, our shoes were taken and we were given old ones."

³ᵃ *a time to kill, and a time to heal*

While it had taken about a week to reach Thorn/Torun by wagon, the return to Wymyschle on foot would take three weeks in the cold weather— "*bei Frost und Schnee*" my grandfather later wrote. As they trudged back to where they had come from, the refugees suffered indignities that my mother recalls. In the cold, soldiers ordered the men and older boys to sit in frozen puddles. Wet, thin clothes turned stiff and stuck to their skin.

One woman with swollen legs had difficulties walking and stayed behind in a barn. The children wouldn't have known why she remained

---

1. Names of cities and towns under the German Occupation are given followed by the Polish names.

behind, except that she couldn't walk. Only recently as we talk together, Anna recalls how in one dark corner of a barn filled with refugees, a woman gave birth. Perhaps it was the same woman. Of the pregnant woman, I read in the family memoir *Unsere Familie*, compiled by Colin Neufeldt (who, like me, is a next-generation witness of former villagers), that after her miscarriage in the hay she caught up with the group.

Henry remembers an old woman who could only walk with a cane so she rode on the wagon. At one point, angered citizens took her off the wagon. The man who led the refugee caravan stepped in to protect her. Blood gushed from the man's head as he tried to intervene, my uncle remembers, but doesn't finish the story. When I ask my mother, she, so small then, remembers an old woman beaten with her own cane.

Henry says the men and teenage boys were beaten. I ask my mother about this, too, and she tells me that Henry was taunted and beaten along with them.

Of these memories, "some of the images never leave you," she now reveals.

It is in Aunt Annie's kitchen, as my son records her story for a school project, that she remembers, "Once, closer to home, we were all taken to a large room." Her memory of trauma is hazy and I surmise the large room could have been a barn or a vacated farmhouse. Her voice softens and lowers. "There we were told we were going to be taken to the woods and shot." My son and I listen silently, as she pauses, then continues. She thinks that someone intervened, and while the details are vague, shards of young Anna's fright still remain, a sudden shudder in my aunt's shoulders. As she talks about this time, she adds, as if to offer a reason why, "the people who did awful things were drunk."

3b *a time to break down, and a time to build up;*

The family limped onward, my mother's oldest sister, Martha, with a sprained ankle, helped by two friends on either side, my grandfather with two-year-old Tilly riding on his shoulders, and the older boys, Henry and John, taking turns carrying baby Bernie in a basket. I envision my grandmother holding the next youngest children, Erna and Ella, by the hand, with Emilie, Bill, and Anna trailing close behind, and all of them shivering, their lips blue.

The River Vistula was already thawing when the refugees were forced to cross back over it because the bridge had been bombed, the ice snapping and crackling like dry twigs beneath an inch of chilling water, soaking their shoes.

"But we didn't fall through," my mother says.

This is the story that my mother and aunts and uncles retell. The Vistula, *die Weichsel,* that runs through Warsaw and Krakow, the sound of splintering ice echoing long after into their futures.

By the time my mother's family reached their village, February 7th, their house had been plundered, stripped of pots, furniture, bedding. The animals that had been abandoned, a few chickens, a pig, all but the cat were gone. The family slept on straw scattered over the floor, and covered themselves with it, too. Even the woodpile for heating the stove had been taken. I surmise that the mice also sought warmth in the straw. But at least the family cat was still there.

[4a]*a time to weep, and a time to laugh;*

My grandmother must have winced at the pulling and tearing, her long braid cut off. Throughout World War II, from Berlin to the Polish villages, and from wherever the German army retreated, this form of shaming was perpetrated on women.

Throughout all the years I knew her, my grandmother wore her long braid, white, usually coiled at the back of her head—sometimes in the morning I saw her with it still slung down her spine before she deftly pinned it up—until her final year in the care-home when her memory had failed her. Then the fine silk strands of hair were cut by her care-givers, and styled into tiny pigtails like a pre-school child's.

My grandfather must have reeled under the bone-crushing force. He was beaten severely by angered Polish citizens. Strangers. Perhaps drunk. They had stormed into the house one night in the dark. Three men. My mother recalls hearing the blows, moans, and thuds; she didn't see what was happening, but she saw her mother crawl out of a window and run to the neighbor's house for help.

Afterwards, in the shadows, the frightened child watched as her mother washed her father's wounds, mother dipping a cloth into a basin and wiping the blood from his face, then holding a tin cup to father's bruised mouth. Erna heard the clatter as he spat out his teeth, hardly any left in his gums. And after he had been tended to, Erna watched as her parents folded their hands and bowed their heads.

My grandfather's stepfather, Mr. Ratzlaff,[2] by now an old man, was also brutally beaten. After a few days he died of his injuries.

As for my grandmother's family members who had taken the other road as masses of refugees were forced to concede the main roadways to retreating columns of troops: her step-mother (aunt) would die, as many older refugees did in the conditions of stress, hunger, freezing temperatures, sickness, or by airplanes strafing the flood of people. Her father Kornelius eventually reached Canada where my grandmother's sisters and half-sisters lived.

[4b]*a time to mourn and a time to dance;*

On March 3rd, my grandfather was arrested as a prisoner of war, and taken to Warsaw until November, when he was transferred to Lodz.[3]

Soon Polish strangers arrived to take over the confiscated farms. Polish people whose own farms had once been seized, displaced earlier in the war when the German people were transferred from other eastern European lands. Characteristic of war was the displacement and relocation of entire populations in the millions. Families, children, the aged, were like flotsam and jetsam in the war's receding and advancing tide.

The ancestral home would be stripped of its ancient thick plank siding; those planks that are the only visible aspect of the house in my old photos. The home of Heinrich and Paulina Unruh and passed on to my grandparents, more than a century of family history ingrained in the wood. Wood used for firewood by others who now also had nothing. Words are all I can reclaim of these terrifying events.

[5a] *a time to cast away stones, and a time to gather stones together;*

Mercifully, the few Polish neighbors in or near Deutsch Wymyschle who knew my grandparents regarded the family as "good people." "We were fortunate that some people in the village knew us, like the man that worked on our farm during the occupation. His family had a boy and a girl," recalls

2. Not to be confused with my grandfather's brother-in-law.

3. Polish name is Lodz. In Prussian times and under the German occupation it was known as Litzmannstadt.

my mother, and she remembers that the man's first name was Bolok. She tries to remember his last name (Sowa?–it seems important to her to remember the name of a kind person). "My parents and others in the village had Polish workers, a *knarsch* (a male farmhand) and *knecht* (a housegirl)." She remembers the name of the girl who had helped with the housework, Mariska, and how she had once taken Erna, age four or five, to her house to visit her parents on her weekend off. "Now we worked for Polish people," my mother says describing this twist of fate.

Strangers occupied the house, but gave my grandmother one room near the barn to live in. It was a *kammer*, a storage room all houses had. In the first years, my grandmother and the five youngest children lived there Otherwise, as was common everywhere now, the displaced slept in barns or out-of-doors.

In her own village, my grandmother washed laundry for food. Tilly and Bernie were left for hours each day in the closed room while my grandmother scoured. Tilly, only three then, still has the memory of her responsibility, the older sister watching after Bernie. One memory is of wandering down the sand road looking for their mother. A Polish man who knew whose children they were, took them back to their room.

During the day, Ella's job, at age four, was to rock another woman's baby, to keep it from crying. Besides fear, this is all Ella remembers of her early years.

Erna, who had just turned six, looked after the chickens for the neighbor, who was the teacher at the school she was not permitted to attend. A common practice was to put duck eggs under the chickens for hatching. But Erna, too young to distinguish between a hatched duckling and chick, was alarmed when the ducklings instinctively headed towards the small pond on the property, so afraid the "chicks" she was supposed to watch would drown.

At first Emilie, seven, also babysat the younger children. Later her job would be to look after horses on a nearby farm without fences.

And at first, because of her sprained ankle, and her ability to knit, the oldest sister, Martha, remained close by, knitting socks and mending. Bill, John, and Henry were all sent to farms to work. Anna, too, was sent further away, to a place where the only food she received was from licking the plates before she washed them.

This part of family history is comprised of fragments, my mother's family members scattered. Each will have their own memories, and some

I can gather from them and sort, not chronologically but narratively. In memory, fear and uncertainty are not sequential.

It's as if all the details were thrown down a dark village well.

[5b]*a time to embrace, and a time to refrain from embracing;*

In January 1946, Erna, not quite seven, was taken in by a young couple in another village a good enough distance away, ten miles perhaps. Her job was to help the wife with household chores, gathering wood, fetching water, and the seemingly terrifying task of herding cows. The pastures were unfenced.

She didn't see her mother for, what seemed to her, months. When her mother came one day, the little girl was overjoyed. I imagine my grandmother making a journey despite her own work and leaving the three younger children, just over five, three and one, for the long walk. When her mother had to say goodbye, my mother remembers how hard she cried; Erna's small thin body wracked by sobs.

I wonder if my grandmother slept that night. This I do know; the next morning she was back and seeing no one home, she took her little daughter with her.

By 1946, Poland permitted Germans in Poland to leave for Germany but proof of family or someone in Germany willing to take them was required for official permission to be granted. Otherwise, ethnic Germans were used as labor. My grandmother and the children tried to leave and took the train, but got only as far as Gostynin. They didn't have the money to bribe the Russian soldiers. Aunt Annie thinks my grandmother may have had one ring for such a purpose, but it wasn't enough.

For a brief time, the farmer with a larger piece of land took on several families to harvest potatoes. My grandmother cooked for the farm laborers. All the workers slept in a barn. My mother remembers it as a good place to work "because each day the children under ten years old received a piece of bread with jam as a treat." This small kindness is remembered. And, after all these years, my mother remembers the name of the family, Syonskosi.

But as winter approached they were asked to leave. Henry and Anna remained working in that area for a time while my grandmother with Martha and John and the younger children, Bill, Emilie, Erna, Ella, Tilly, and Bernie returned to Wymyschle; this time another Polish family whose name my mother also remembers, Sikora, took in my Grandmother and her youngest children.

As a child my mother wondered why theirs was the only Mennonite family left behind in the village. She told me my grandmother would always remember how she, Erna, repeatedly asked her during that time, "*wann fahren wir raus?*" When will we leave?

When?

[6a]*a time to seek, and a time to lose;*

These years were completely absorbed with survival. "From 1945 until we left Poland I never slept indoors," Henry recalls. He slept only in barns and haystacks and worked on farms solely for food, and at times there wasn't any. Food was simply potatoes from the fields, roasted in a campfire. Or perhaps orchard fruit. Often rotting vegetables and fruit. Sometimes, one of the workers would let a hen out to lay eggs in the grass, so the laborers could find and eat them. Henry spoke better Polish than German. He thought being taken into labor was the punishment for his Germanness.

My mother recalls that her head was shaved because of the lice. Erna had sores from scratching it. "Oma put *naft* (kerosene from the lamps) on our heads to kill the lice, then she tied a kerchief over," my mother tells me. The little girls and Bernie, heads shorn, scabbed, then bound and smelling of kerosene. The older children could come home once in a while if they could manage the distance. "John got boils. Oma lanced them when he came home," my mother adds.

She remembers, "Everyone wore a black patch on their clothing" Henry remembers the patch that he was, along with all the *Volksdeutsch* in Poland, required to wear as identification; the patch was actually white and black. All the Germans over the age of five wore a patch on their left chest, a 6-centimeter by 6-centimeter white diamond with a thick black letter N to signify their undesirable identity. My mother must be remembering the thick black letter, 4 centimeters high and wide, and 1 centimeter thick.[4]

"The Russians let us take them off, which in reality protected us," Henry tells me. All throughout these years my uncle spoke only Polish, fluently; without a trace of German otherness.

---

4. Marchlewski, "Hollanders During the World War II and their Post-War Situation," 10.

⁶ᵇ*a time to keep, and a time to cast away;*

From the beginning of the war, the Mennonite Central Committee (MCC), a relief agency of Mennonites in North America, had attempted to help the Mennonites in Poland.[5] MCC had originally formed in 1920 to provide famine relief to Russia and help to Mennonites in Russia to leave following the revolution and in advance of Stalin's Communist economic plans. These "plans" were literally arrests of anyone accused of being an enemy of the state, land-owners, and religious believers, to populate an extensive system of labor camps that became known as the Gulag. (In this manner, the Soviet Union attempted to become a leading industrial nation through forced labor. This is the time my father lived through in Ukraine). In Poland, as early as 1940, the MCC was permitted by the German Foreign ministry to assist Polish citizens and prisoners of war in German camps, and work closely with the Red Cross to assist these displaced people.

Later in 1946, the MCC opened a relief unit in Poland near Danzig. The aim was to provide agricultural and material assistance to the Polish people who had suffered in the war. But MCC's work in Poland was growing more difficult as US and Soviet relations began to weaken. And, unofficially, MCC's goal was to contact any remaining Mennonites in the area.

Among the MCC documents from the spring of 1948 is a report submitted by Menno Fast to MCC headquarters in Basil, Switzerland. Fast was an MCC worker sent to Poland to visit farms that had been given North American tractors by the United Nations Relief and Rehabilitation Administration. As he traveled throughout Poland visiting farms, he became aware of the presence of Mennonites and began to record their names and whereabouts. In his report to MCC he observed:

> The Polish authorities have considered (the Mennonites) as Germans and have dealt with them accordingly: that is, they have disowned them of their properties and placed most of them under the administration of labor camps where they are forced to work, usually without wages. In a few rare cases they may be working privately for peasants who pay them subsistence wages. Others find themselves in prison where they are practically cut off from the rest of the world.[6]

5. Schroeder Thiessen and Showalter, *A Life Displaced*, 9.

6. Ibid., 21–22.

[7a]*a time to tear and a time to sew;*

My mother vaguely recalls a truck with a canopy driving into the village. It was from the MCC. Tilly remembers that only she and Bernie were home when someone came to the door.

The children in the village received scribblers and pencils. Shoes were handed out. The pair Erna was given pinched her feet, but she still wore them.

By July 1948, the North American MCC worker, Menno Fast, had compiled a list of Mennonites in Poland. He obtained the names and addresses primarily from relatives in Germany and North America, and from those within refugee camps who knew about others who had not been seen, or heard from. Is this how the relief organization knew my grandmother was still in the village in Poland? Did relatives, who by now had made it to Germany, tell MCC workers that they had not been heard from; had been turned back?

Imagine what it is like; to know you've been searched for, and found.

Miraculously, in the fall of 1948, with the help of MCC workers who had been assisting refugees throughout Eastern Europe, the family procured the proper travel documents. My mother thinks back to how the children, scattered in different locations, all convened for the transport to Germany, and proposes that my grandmother, knowing where each was, had managed to get word to them. She thinks my grandmother probably walked to see each one. She had tried to visit her children on Sundays. Or perhaps the MCC truck had found and notified each one. At last. My grandmother with her ten surviving children would leave what had been their home place.

On November 9, 1948, the last group of fifty Germans from the area boarded the MCC truck.[7] Among them were members of the Schroeder family. They first stopped in Warsaw, and in a large Catholic church they were processed, along with all those leaving Poland. Anna recalls that among them were Jewish people; those who had come out of hiding. No doubt, also those who had survived the camps.

On the way out of Poland to Germany, when the train stopped in Lodz, their father was able to meet them at the train station for a brief reunion. However, as a German, he would still be detained for years, sentenced to labor for reparations. They traveled with other refugees by train,

7. Marchlewski, "Hollanders During the World War II and their Post-War Situation," 1.

in boxcars, sitting in straw. Crossing the border from Poland into Germany, along the way the Soviets tried to convince the young people to remain in the Soviet zone. One old woman advised Henry that it would be worse to stay, it would be better to go on to the British zone.

My grandmother and her children were able to reach a refugee camp run by the MCC in Gronau, Germany near the Dutch-German border, just before Christmas 1948.

The entire trip from Poland took six to eight weeks.

The Polish government asked the MCC to leave the country in 1949. A curtain of silence closed around Poland until the 1970s.

MCC re-established ties with Poland during the 1970s, bringing farmers and students to North America for educational and cultural exchange. From 1979 through 1983, MCC provided relief aid throughout Poland's economic crises. Today the MCC, represented by Mennonite groups from Amish to Evangelical, with Mennonite communities in countries throughout North America, Europe, India, China, Lebanon, El Salvador, Mozambique, and elsewhere, is an organization that holds a special place in the lives of Mennonites. Through its broad volunteer and donor base—comprised of former World War II refugees and others—MCC raises millions of dollars annually at relief sales in an effort to continue to supply material aid to those in need the world over.

Today, Syria, where eleven million people are displaced by violence, is the biggest crisis response MCC has undertaken, including assisting the refugees of World War II.

7b*a time to keep silence, and a time to speak;*

While Poland was a home place for my grandparents and their ancestors, and *Deutsch* Wymyschle was a village established a century or more before, from much older settlements, the truth is, what was "a time for up-rooting" became a beginning. At the same time, I am cognizant that home place, whole communities, and a particular way of life, ended forever in Poland.

There is a time to be silent and a time to speak. After trauma, sometimes the silence is healing. But if silence is because of fear or shame, it is destructive, says a favorite poet of mine, Gregory Orr. After all this time, I'll never know my grandparents' thoughts when they were young and in

Poland, and all that their story entailed, in the beginning, during and at the end of the war.

I think of each of my grandmothers who never spoke about those difficult years. My paternal grandmother, who had fled the Soviet Union during the war, died when I was quite young. My maternal grandmother lived a long life, and yet I never asked her about the past, in Poland, nor did she speak of it with me.

Nonetheless, in my mother's large immigrant family, the quality of their silence was not a hush.

[8a]*a time to love and a time to hate;*

Among my grandparents, my aunts and uncles and all my cousins, what took the place of talking about the past was the bustle of starting over and living, of gathering together with one another and talking (and in my mother's large family, interrupting each other) about matters of the present day. My grandparents, together with relatives and friends, those who experienced youth and happiness in Poland, chose amongst each other to remember better days. And I remember how content they seemed.

There is a story about the family pictures, and I wonder, as I look at the ones I have of my grandparents as young people—their wedding portrait in 1923, or the young family in Poland, childhood pictures of David, the last pictures of him in 1943—what are the stories I'm missing? The older girls had carried the family pictures in a handbag and hung them on the wagon as they fled; the handbag stolen from the wagon along the way. But my grandmother's sisters must have taken copies with them when they immigrated to Canada in the 1920s. My grandmother must have also sent her sisters photographs of the family with David when he was last home on furlough. I try to imagine what it was like for her to have her photographs, symbols of that which been stolen from her life, given back to her.

[8b]*a time for war and a time for peace.*

After tearing down, there is a time to build; after weeping, a time to laugh; after mourning, a time to dance; after scattering stones, a time to gather them like memories into stories. Solomon also writes that there is a time to embrace and a time to refrain from embracing, a time to seek and a time to give up, a time to keep and a time to throw away. Perhaps what we refrain from embracing, what we give up, what we throw away, is an attachment to the past. Or the impulse to hold on to misfortune and misery. There is a time to tear . . .

There is a time to sew or mend. A time, after silence, to speak. There is a time to love, which is also a time to hate things like injustice. And after a time of war there is a time for peace. But grief is a long migration and the act of gathering various and fragmented memories—my mother's, her brothers' and sisters'—can be done only after time has passed. Even now, I marvel at the capacity of memories to hold truth; the experiences of brothers and sisters of different ages, their details over time snatched along the way, like stolen photographs and a confiscated wagon, but then, one day recovered. Not the genuine artifacts, but a true depiction of them.

⁓

Concerning the district of Gostynin where the family village was located:

> Mass departures of people devoid of Polish citizenship took place between June and November 1947. On 5 November 1947 a deportation transport was organized for 1,200 Germans, mainly mothers with children and old people. After this action, 2,000 Germans still remained on the territory of the Gostynin *poviat*. The last ones left in 1948. That year the history of colonists, not only on the territory of Mazovia so tangled and tragic, ended.[8]

8. Marchlewski, "Hollanders During World War II, and Their Post-War Situation," 12. Furthermore, in the mass expulsion of Germans in Eastern Europe under the Allied agreement, millions were sent to labor camps throughout the Soviet Union. Of those who survived, the last were released in 1955. These stories are now becoming known.

Quiet

8

Crochet

(or, a story of the immigrant family)

A yarn: a strand of fiber.

In the winter evenings when the sunlight has faded, my mother crochets an afghan. Occasionally, she'll knit one, and as she knits and purls, the yarn flows as a river through a valley. But usually, she'll crochet. Her hands work the yarn, and row by row a mantle of color and texture grows. From a grey-blue strand, she crochets a blanket of ocean. Then a rolling field in soft shades of sage, or wheat and rye. Night after night, my mother's hands work the fiber, back and forth, the yarn's migration over an expanse, each blanket framed with a chorded edge, rows of crossed double crochet stitches that alternate with a row of single stitches. The border becomes both beginning and ending; framework and context.

As for fiber art, my own early knowledge of knitting went only as far as the stocking stitch. I don't know how to hold a crochet hook, how to guide the hook and hold the yarn in place keeping the tension even; how to wrap the yarn and pull up a loop; skillfully, patiently unraveling a long, cohesive strand. My mother insists that her work isn't anything special. Whether by needle or hook, how to vary the pattern, she says, is easy. She understates this artistry. The textures and motifs of design are subtle but no less integral to the ultimate beauty of the work when it is complete.

It's an acquired skill, this connecting and joining—of knowing just when to drop or add a stitch.

~

Yarn: a long story with incredible events.

Like a ball of wool, slowly unraveled, fashioned into a pattern and framed by a corded edge, is family narrative—from one long strand like a crochet chain (insert hook, yarn over). It's an immigrant story, one particular story among many. The arc of such a narrative begins in another country, has its conflict and climax in war, its denouement in starting over. And typically, the telling begins only long after such an ending. Often it will be the next generation that fashions the text out of the tangled yarn.

There are only a few photographs from the past. In this particular one, my grandmother sits at the center in a black knit sweater, grey straight skirt, thick dark stockings, and sensible shoes, all donated by the refugee agency: she, like the nucleus of an atom, and clustered around her, in light cotton dresses, in matching pairs, are her six daughters. The two youngest girls lean from their seats and nestle into her sides. The little girls wear short-sleeved dresses and leotards, so it must be spring. Eight-year-old Ella's thick stocking is torn at the right knee and will need mending. Erna has just turned ten years old, waif-like and shadow-eyed in the photo. She stands behind her mother, hand on her shoulder, and I get a renewed sense of how great a comfort the presence of a mother must have been. Perhaps for a displaced refugee child, if not for most young children, it is not a house or a place that is home to her; rather, it is her mother.

Since December, just before Christmas 1948, they have been clothed, fed, and settled in the refugee camp in Gronau, Germany, near the border to Poland. I think the photo was taken in March 1949, a conjecture based on a second photograph and what I know about that one.

It is a similar photo of my grandfather seated among the four sons, the same building in the background. His face is angular, cheeks hollow, eyes sunken, and he looks old except that he still has a dark, thick shock of hair. In his second-hand suit, he is flanked by the two youngest boys, also seated on wooden stools. The smallest one, Bernie, age five, wearing a pullover sweater, and stockings beneath short pants, is pulling at the leg of his short pants. Bill wears trousers and a button-down sweater. My grandfather cups his hands over his knees. The oldest sons, John and Henry, are dressed in suits and ties, and stand behind, their arms and hands hanging at their sides. They all seem stiff and awkward. My grandfather had just arrived in the refugee camp (in March 1949) after being released from internment in Poland. What doesn't escape me about that photo is how emaciated my grandfather is, and how foreign he seems among his sons, especially five year-old Bernie, who was only five months old when his father was taken.

At first sent to a prison camp in Warsaw after he was arrested on March 3rd, 1945, my grandfather was later transferred to Lodz, in November 1945, to work in a wool factory, *Woll-Wasch und Spinn Fabrik*. His task was to wash the wool before it was spun onto spools.

These two photos, among the others, are like knots in a skein. I have to pause, inspect, work them through and unravel the particulars within.

∿

The war has left its gaping holes. Unravel memory; then knit, purl, knit, purl . . .

Pictures of David reveal an adolescent with dark and placid eyes. The telegram had informed my grandparents that he had been killed on the Eastern front (*gefallen im Osten, den 25.10.43, 65 km, Lidlich Saparascha*).

The older siblings remember their brother David and describe him as a soft-spoken boy, a patient older brother who helped with farm and household chores. To help his mother, he patiently brushed and braided his little sisters' hair. David, they remember, could knit and spent winter evenings darning the family's socks and knitting scarves. When Martha was old enough, she began knitting, too, then Anna. The girls were knitting by the age of six, and by eight they were making socks and mittens, the muffled clicking of knitting needles in nimble fingers. Any sweater with a hole in it was unraveled and the wool reused. No wool was wasted.

A few years ago, when I began to ask more specific questions about my mother's childhood, she produced a small, cloth bag. The little purse was stitched together by hand and closed with a snap. On the front of the coarse brown woolen fabric, a child stitched her initials, *E.S.*, in pastel green yarn. Little flowers or clovers—four petals each—embroidered in cornflower blue, navy, and black; this is one of the crafts the children made in the refugee camp; each of the younger girls—Emilie, Erna, and Ella—would have made one.

Inside this little bag, however, wrapped in tissue paper, are astonishing original photos. Small vintage photographs of young foot soldiers in training exercises, setting up camp, relaxing by a river, digging trenches, marching along dirt roads. Pictures that once belonged to David, all that was tangibly left to remember him by. These must have been concealed by my grandmother during those years in Poland; keepsakes kept secret, for if they had been discovered, it's plausible she might have been killed.

My mother has given me another keepsake from that time. I now keep it in my office on my bookshelf: a small basket she wove at age ten in the refugee camp. "There was a children's choir, planned activities, and crafts. Even Sunday school and church." Life felt organized and secure, something my mother had not experienced since the age of four or five, and something her youngest siblings could not remember feeling at all before this. The older siblings worked in the *Gerhard von Delden* factory in Gronau, a *Spuehlerei* where cotton thread was manufactured.

Together with other children in the camp, my mother wove the little basket from brown, orange, red, and beige strands that spiral out from a center, a circumference of fifteen rows, and each one bonded to the next by filament.

Past and the present are attached by an imperceptible thread, and within time's circumference, endings and beginnings merge.

To begin, pull a length of yarn and tie yarn on to crochet hook.

Right after their reunification, in April 1949, the family applied to immigrate to Canada.

Eight of the twelve family members were found to have TB spots on their lungs. Erna, Ella, and Tilly were hospitalized. My mother remembers the nurse in the hospital, and the children's choir director, a young Mennonite woman from Canada named Martha Thiessen.

In 1950, the family was again examined and rejected for immigration. My mother and her older sister Emilie were sent to *Schloss Reder*, an *Erholungs Heim*, a camp where sick and undernourished children recovered. The girls were fed well and napped in the sunshine outdoors on the grass. Meanwhile, the family was relocated to another rural town, into shared housing. Siblings Anna and Bill worked threshing in the fields.

Insert crochet hook into yarn. Loop over. Pull through. Continue, stitch by stitch, row by row.

In 1951, the family was again called to the camp in Gronau for examinations. Tilly still had spots on her lungs. The family considered its options:

leaving the oldest daughter, Martha with the youngest, Tilly, while the rest of the family went on ahead. Or immigrating to Uruguay, a country not as restrictive as Canada. It was settled, the family would stay together and go to Uruguay. The oldest son, Henry, who by now had a job and had made friends, wanted to remain in Germany. But, at age twenty-four, he agreed to emigrate with his family—and while they awaited transport to Uruguay, once again they were called in for an examination. This time, all were cleared. They could go to Canada where sponsoring relatives in Alberta awaited them.

An ending becomes a beginning.

The photograph on the steps of the immigration office in Bremen, in 1951, is my favorite family photograph. On the first step of the building, my grandfather stands, hat in hand, his left hand in the pocket jacket of a three-piece suit, complete with white shirt and tie, like a gentleman; my grandmother stands beside him on the step, in a knitted skirt and sweater, hands behind her back. The clothing is, of course, second-hand from the relief organization. Behind my grandparents, like stair steps, are the ten children in order of age. The happy look on their faces exudes hope. The people lined up behind them in the photo, also immigrants, mostly young men, and one couple with a baby, look at the camera, too, but the lens seems fixed on this anomaly; such a large family together, after survival—seemingly whole. As penniless refugees, the family of twelve took on a travel debt totaling $3,000. Of that $3,000, it cost $2,800 to leave, and $200 for a new start which they would receive upon arrival in Halifax.

With its transport of refugees, the *MS Nelly* sailed from the port of Bremen on November 12th 1951, to Le Havre, France, where two hundred more passengers boarded the ship, before setting out on a calm sea for Canada. By November 15th, the water grew rougher, and the next day it was stormy. A sea in chevron patterns like my mother's afghans, swelling white crests, grey, deep blue, darkening to black. It seemed an endless expanse to cross, until, on November 22nd, at five o'clock in the morning, the lights on the shores of Halifax greeted them in the sunrise, and the family disembarked to board the train west.

After all these years, the brothers and sisters don't remember much about the Atlantic crossing. Except for John, then twenty-two, who had taken a few notes on the weather, whether the sea was stormy or calm, how many minutes the clock was pushed back each day, and who in the family was sea-sick during the ten-day voyage.

There are no starry details concerning Martha, age twenty, who met her future husband Gerhardt in the camp in Bremerhaven, a young man alone, leaving Germany behind and who had also traveled aboard the *Nelly*. This could be attributed to her shyness, but perhaps more to the fact that young immigrants didn't spend time romanticizing. They simply got on with the task of starting over.

My grandfather threw his pipe overboard. "He knew the relatives in Canada wouldn't like it that he smoked," my mother remembers.

The train stopped first in Winnipeg where familiar faces from the village in Poland greeted them at the station. Kindnesses would be remembered and named. In Calgary, they met their Canadian sponsors, Mr. and Mrs. C. Toews from Linden, Alberta, and also reunited with more families from Poland, some who had left Poland before the war (my grandfather's sister, Frieda, and her husband, David, who lived in Olds, Alberta). They were reunited with those who had also fled the Mennonite settlement, Wymyschle, sometime in January 1945 six years earlier, but who had not been turned back by Russian soldiers and had somehow made it through to Germany. My grandfather's half-brother, Erhard, with his family had made it to Canada in 1948.

Before the end of November, with the work ethic of new immigrants, the family settled on the farm of Mr. and Mrs. W. Oxland, and began paying off their three-hundred-dollar *per person* travel debt through farm labor and domestic work. At eighteen, Anna looked after the Oxland twins, surmising that Mrs. Oxland chose her because Martha would likely marry and leave sooner. When my mother sometimes visited her sister at the house, Mrs. Oxland gave Erna soft white bread spread with *Miracle Whip* for a snack. Mrs. Oxland even offered to give her piano lessons, but the woman's health was unsteady, and so, too, was their lesson schedule. Martha went to work in Calgary.

Along with Anna, and their parents, Henry worked on the Oxland's farm and remembers, while combining oats, barley, and wheat in the spring, having to stop the machinery often to pull the mice out. John found work on other farms, then construction work in Calgary. Bill went to live and help on Uncle Ben Ratzlaff's farm, and started school. The younger ones stayed with their parents, helped with chores and began school. Erna, Bill, and Emilie were placed together in a grade five/six class, and were taught the grade one curriculum by their teacher.

My mother says she doesn't remember much about their first Christmas in Canada in 1951, but she remembers her cousin Hedy gave her a pair of used ice skates and the girls skated on the pond at the farm.

Each Sunday afternoon, after church, was filled with visiting relatives.

My grandparents and the older children paid off the entire debt within ten months, the five older siblings, Henry, John, Martha, Anna, and Bill each paying for the younger siblings, Emilie, Erna, Ella, Tilly, and Bernie. And by that second Christmas in Canada, each of the older siblings was matched with a younger one and bought a gift for him or her. My mother, who would become a fashionable dresser, has never forgotten the navy blue skirt and pink blouse John gave her that year, 1952, when she was thirteen.

By then, as children will, my mother was already acculturating. The summer of 1952, Aunt Frieda and Uncle Dave invited Erna to come to stay with them in Olds. My mother was inclined to see the invitation as an opportunity for some time to herself, and, perhaps, for some attention. She helped in the kitchen, and Aunt Frieda gave her children's books to read. They listened to story hour on the radio after lunch. Older cousin Anne, who worked in Calgary, even cut Erna's braids off and gave her short hair a perm, though my mother admits she didn't know how to manage or style this new look. And while as a young teen, she may have been pulling at independence or seeking a loosening from the past, Aunt Frieda taught my mother, who already knew how to knit, how to crochet.

The differences between knitting and crochet, besides the obvious one of using two needles versus one hook, are structural and worth noting.

In knitting, a dropped stitch can unravel a fabric. But a dropped stitch in crochet rarely interferes with the piece. This is because in crochet, there is only one "live" stitch on the hook, while in knitting, an entire row of stitches is simultaneously active. Additionally, the looping in crochet (insert hook, loop over one, or two, or more depending on the pattern) is more complex and unlikely to come loose under stress. Each stitch is supported by the corresponding stitch above and below, and conversely supports the stitches on either side of it. Thus, if a stitch in a finished piece breaks, the stitches around it remain intact.[1] I often think about what it is concerning my mother's immigrant family that has kept it together despite dropped

---

1. Wikipedia, *Crochet*.

stitches, imperfections and time. It's something inherently structural, I realize, like the way each stitch in crochet is supported by those on either side, above and below, held in place, even when there is a tear.

My grandparents made the decision to move to British Columbia where there were more opportunities to obtain a small farm of their own. Alberta winters were cold, and more land to farm was required than in BC. Uncle Erhard's family had already moved to a Mennonite farming community called Arnold on the Sumas Prairie, where other Wymyschle people were now living. And so on May 21st, 1953, the Schroeder family arrived at the train station in nearby Mission, British Columbia, and were greeted by more families they knew from the Old World. They stayed with another family near the Mennonite church on Marion Road in Arnold, and on July 2nd, 1954, moved into their very own home at 588 Marion Road, which they bought from Mr. Peter Schulz for $7,500. They made a down payment of $1,500 and, with the help of the older children, repaid that, plus made payments of $1,000 at 5 percent interest per year.

In 1967, when I was five years old, my grandparents sold the farm. I still have memories of the large garden and fruit trees, rows of raspberries, milking barn, and shed where the family butchered. But all my grandparents' children had by then moved from home and though the family came on weekends to help, and helped with crops in summer, the work was too much. My grandparents purchased a small lot on Countess Street in Clearbrook. A royal sounding address for my grandparents from a Polish village. Clearbrook would be a Mennonite enclave, and here, too, was Martha Thiessen, the young nurse from Canada, who in 1947 worked with the children in the refugee camp in Germany. She was one of the many Canadian Mennonites who volunteered in the huge relief effort to assist refugees from Europe. In my grandmother's later years, Martha Thiessen would visit her, commenting to my mother and aunts what a remarkable woman their mother, my grandmother, was, remembering her without a husband, with ten children, who had arrived at the refugee camp from Poland.

My grandparents lived in the house on Countess Street in Clearbrook for a decade, until my grandfather's stroke. Together the old couple moved to a seniors' home, operated by the Mennonite Benevolent Society, and which was then a community of their immigrant peers.

Crochet

My grandfather died in 1982. I remember that my widowed grandmother used to knit and crochet and how, in her last years, her memories began to vanish like dropped stitches.

My mother and her siblings, now in their seventies and eighties, gather often during the year for each of their birthdays. In summer there's an annual family picnic, at Christmas we rent out a church basement or gym, and we, the Canadian-born cousins, with our children, and now even our grandchildren, still come, identifying ourselves as *family*. The members of a particular family—each of us held in place by one another as if by a stitch.

Now that the aunts and uncles are older, they talk about the past. But as my mother admits, she has forgotten many of the details, and doesn't want to remember certain ones. As with the fiber art of crochet, a dropped stitch in story can be deliberate, and does not necessarily cause the material to deteriorate. Memories of the past fade. For some, traumatic memories are blocked. And each family member's memory of a shared event will differ. But family narrative only has strands of memory on which to rely. Holding the yarn in tension, we wrap it, pull up a loop, each stitch held in place by others around it, creating a pattern, fashioning something to wrap ourselves in, or to pass along—to remember and to release.

9

Between Worlds

(Return to Poland, 1973)

My father built a house for my grandparents on a street with other immigrants from war-torn villages for neighbors. Our family lived close by
and my mother dropped in often to do errands with them, me in tow. She
would drive them to Dr. Giesbrecht for check-ups, to Funk's or Penner's
Supermarkets for groceries, and to Neufeldt's Shoes for shoe repairs. Or
we'd just stop by for visits. After greeting my grandmother, if my grandfather was not upstairs I'd wander to the basement. I might discover his
dentures, a disembodied grin of synthetic pink gums, floating in a glass left
by the sink in the basement washroom. And there in the basement, I could
find my toothless grandfather napping on a hot summer afternoon, or, if I
visited after school, in front the black-and-white TV with rabbit ears, his
folding chair set in front of the screen, his shoulders shaking with silent
laughter.

It used to be, among the older people in the Mennonite Church, that
owning a television was frowned upon; it was "of the world." Against the
rules. Traditionally, Mennonites were to be "in the world" but not of it. But
by the late 1960s when my grandparents moved off the farm into town after

their children were grown, most with families of their own, the reason my grandparents' TV was in the basement was because it was a comfortable place where Opa could watch comfortably, and undisturbed.

I don't know if my grandfather comprehended a word, or if, perhaps, this was how he learned the extremely limited English vocabulary he possessed, but the shows he watched were sit-coms. Comedy doesn't often require subtitles. There were two shows he tuned into, each one ran from the early or mid-sixties to the early seventies. Perhaps these two particular pop-culture shows somehow made my grandfather feel somewhat less a stranger in a new country, less on the margin.

And I don't know why a half-hour comedy show about a prison camp and Nazis wouldn't seem offensive to a German, or *Volksdeutscher*, from Poland, one who had lived through such a time, had even been a POW. Perhaps the reason Opa tuned in daily to *Hogan's Heroes* was because this show was an alternate version of that war. Ridiculous. A farce. He laughed at these affable Allied prisoners, Hogan the captain played by Bob Crane, Corporals LeBeau and Newkirk and the others, especially the fat and bungling German Sergeant of the Guards, Schulz, whose line or catchphrase "I know *nuthink*, I see *nuthink*, I hear *NUTHINK*" always set my plump grandfather to chuckling in his chair.

The show, with its crude characterizations, was a mockery of the Nazis. This my grandfather would have understood. He may not have understood the dialogue, but the plot line was always stock and easy to follow. The prisoners use the camp as a base of operations for sabotage against Nazi Germany and to smuggle prisoners from under Colonel Klink's monocle. Their wily ways keep the clueless Klink in charge of the camp so that the POWs can continue their improbable shenanigans and win the war.

Werner Klemperer, who played Klink, won the series its two Emmy awards for outstanding supporting actor in a comedy.[1]

Much later, in 2002, *TV Guide* would rate the show the fifth worst TV series of all time for trivializing the suffering of real life POWs, more so for presenting a comedic take on prison camps in the Third Reich, and especially so when considering the victims of the Holocaust.[2]

My grandfather also tuned in to *The Beverly Hillbillies*. It ran from 1962 until 1971 and, according to Nielsen Media Research, remains one

1. Wikipedia, *Hogans Heros*.

2. Wikipedia, *Hogans Heros*: Cosgrove-Mather, The Worst TV Shows Ever." http://www.cbsnews.com/stories/2002/07/12/entertainment/51505CBS News.

of the most-watched television series of all-time.[3] A poor rural family is transplanted from the Ozarks to Beverly Hills—a similar story arc to my grandparents' uprooting from a rural country village in Poland, with dirt roads and no indoor plumbing, to a brand new house in a paved subdivision, on wealthy-sounding Countess Street, in Canada. My grandparents were in their late sixties and early seventies themselves, having been born at the cusp of the century. Now, like Granny Daisy May Moses and her son-in-law, Jed Clampett, they were starting over.

In both the TV family and my grandparents' family, the children acculturated rapidly. Despite my grandfather's strict rules about dress, in line with the code of modesty in the Mennonite church the family attended, as they left home the girls back-combed their hair into great hives sprayed to perfection with "Adorn," went sleeveless with their short skirts, panty hose and heels, as coquettish yet as innocent as Elly May.

The show was considered low-brow by critics. Oh, well. We were an immigrant family whose second language was English. As a child I made the subconscious connection between my grandparents from elsewhere and the TV Clampett family. They felt familiar, so this might have been the appeal of the show for my grandfather, too. I sat with him watching the hillbillies' antics in their fancy new Beverly Hills neighborhood, and we giggled in the basement together.

The Clampetts were a rags-to-riches story, analogous to the immigrant experience. In an alternate TV world, Opa could have played the role of Jed-the-mountaineer, with little formal education but a lot of common sense and a good nature, if Jed were a Mennonite from Wymyschle Poland, not a hillbilly from Bugtussle. Oma would have had the role of Granny, no-nonsense and able to make a meal from a road-killed opossum if necessary, which is to say food in my grandmother's house was rustic Polish/Mennonite—plentiful and never wasted. And though their little house on a town lot was not opulent, it was their mansion.

And while I was at home in this in-between world of my grandparents, and these post-war times were fraught with more cultural change than I, singing *Blowin' in the Wind* in elementary school, could possibly understand, I had the company of two old people I loved and visited often, and afternoon television. Although *Happy Days*, the wildly popular show about middle-class teens in a still-conservative world would not premier until the

---

3. Wikipedia, *The Beverly Hillbillies.*

next year, 1974, I could have sung its theme song, "these happy days are yours and mine, oh happy days."

~

My grandfather returned to Poland in the summer of 1973, almost twenty years after he had arrived in Canada. As a child, I never thought to ask him why he would go back. And I didn't know it then, but just before this time, in 1970, then West German chancellor, Willy Brandt, traveled to Poland on a State visit, and knelt in silence before a monument at the Warsaw Ghetto. Then, just eight years old, I wouldn't have known what had happened here.

This return trip to Poland would be my grandfather's first travel experience *not* as a refugee and, at seventy-three years old, his first airplane ride. He traveled with four other men, all of them also once residents of the village in Poland. Poland was under the Communist government, a puppet state of the Soviet regime—the regime they had tried to flee from, unsuccessfully, as its army's front advanced at the end of the war. In hindsight, I marvel at the pluck of these oldsters returning to their former homeplace.

My grandfather wrote about the trip for the *Mennonitische Rundschau*, the German-language paper with news of all things Mennonite. The paper began as the *Nebraska Ansieder* published in 1878 but by mid-1880 had changed its name to signify the larger community that it was serving; the paper was a link between family members, communities and congregations wherever Mennonites were settled. The *Mennonitische Rundschau* was one of the longest-running German-language papers in North America, ceasing publication in 2007. In July 1973, my grandfather described the mundane details of their momentous and newsworthy trip back to the homeland. The dinner on the airplane, the "*schmackhaftes abendbrot*," might have been one of the few times Opa had not eaten in his or in someone else's home. Wonder of wonders, he proclaimed it "a tasty dinner," and served on an airplane no less! And because they arrived in Germany at night, driving from Frankfurt to Bielefeld, where my grandmother's oldest sister had settled, not wanting to wake their hosts, this would have been the first time my grandfather slept in a hotel. With a brother-in-law from Bielefeld joining them, the menfolk then traveled by train to Warsaw, through the *Bundes Republik*, over the border into the *DDR*, then across the border into Poland.

My grandfather writes (in German) "there is nothing more to see of the war's destruction, everything is rebuilt and clean." Between the lines are these facts: the Polish capital, Warsaw, was deliberately annihilated by Nazi troops in 1944 in retaliation for the resistance shown by the Polish people. From 1945 to 1966, the Poles reconstructed the Old Town from the ruins. I later would learn from a Polish guide that the people rebuilt their city as an act of resistance, and the Russians were angered by this, but the Poles spun the enterprise into a story about the "people working together," and so the Russians relented. I would also discover that ethnic Germans imprisoned for reparations labored to reconstruct Warsaw.

"The people are well-dressed, and are friendly and helpful. And," adds my grandfather, "we haven't seen any women or girls in mini-skirts, or young men with long hair and beards." I don't suppose so in a Communist country! But that certainly made an impression on him. My grandfather notes that he and his friend sat in a park with the luggage while their companions went off to sight-see around the Old Town and, "*Habe viel uber unsere langhaarigen and bartigen Manner nachgedacht* (thought a lot about our long-haired and bearded men)."

Who knows if long-haired men with beards and girls in mini-skirts brought to Opa's mind the rebelliousness of youth, or something more? At this time, the Vietnam War wouldn't end for another year. Perhaps my grandfather saw the images of protest and resistance on television. What would he have thought to himself, alone in the little room in the basement? *But*, some people would think, *Mennonites are known for social activism and resistance to war.* He wouldn't have understood most of the news in English as spoken by Walter Cronkite on *CBS Evening News*, but he read newspapers in German. He wasn't uninformed. I wonder today what more he thought about, and didn't write, as he sat on the park bench on the corner of Marszalkovska and Jeruzolimska streets, where most of the beautiful homes had been destroyed in the Warsaw uprising, the "wedding cake structure" called the Joseph Stalin Palace of Culture and Science in their place.

As I picture my grandfather in the park in Warsaw, I remember how he enjoyed sitting outside his house on a sunny day, in a lawn chair, or on the bench under the kitchen window, Mr. Schmidt, the neighbor, his companion. He loved to visit while my grandmother busied herself in the garden in the backyard, or in the kitchen. My diabetic grandfather with his bad leg, and peppermints in his pocket for the sugar low. Here in Warsaw, dressed in his Sunday suit, white shirt and tie, wearing a hat, he was content to remain and watch over the luggage. Of course, as he waited for his friends, he would have had a picture in his mind of the rubble and ash, for he had been here, at the close of the war. He had been taken to Warsaw following his arrest, after the capitulation of the German army, and spent nine months in a camp before being transferred to Lodz for another four years. A civilian prisoner of war under Poland, the conditions a far cry from the studio-lot *Luftwaffe Stalag 13*, with its constant artificial winters in the California sun.

~

From Warsaw it is a few hours by train and car to the Mennonite settlement, the homeplace. The men took the train to the station nearest the community. Arriving late, they checked into the Hotel *Turysta* (for what else would a Soviet-era hotel be called?), quite probably the only hotel in town for foreign tourists. And just who are the tourists? My grandfather notes in his article that the guests were a bus-load each of American and British travelers, but were not, like these older "Canadian" men, returning to their birthplaces. In the morning they felt "well-rested," as my grandfather writes, "for the day, after so many years, we have looked forward to, the return to our dear homeplace, in peace; to where we were born, and grew up, and had to leave. All things have turned out and we are grateful with all our heart."

On the first day, the men took a taxi to Kazun, the former Mennonite settlement, where they met people they recognized from long ago, and noted that the church was a house to three families now. The second and third day (Friday and Saturday), they visited the villages of their birth, and the nearby town Gabin, a center of commerce, where they used to shop and trade, and where once was a vibrant Jewish community.

Although my grandfather is back for the first and only time since he was forced from his home in 1945, two of the other men have not been back since leaving for Canada in the 1930s. And here, in the old homeplace, the village *Wymysle* (as it is now spelled in Polish), my grandfather reconnected with his old friend, Reinhold Wegert, to whom he had kept writing from Canada, slipping paper dollars into the envelope before pressing it shut. He spent the night in his friend's home, the house that had once belonged to my grandmother's family members, and describes waking in the morning to the rural scenes from his upper window: "the men in the fields, the women setting their milk cans on the dirt street to be collected by the milk wagon."

Despite such scenes of village life that had not changed much from when my grandfather lived here, his father-in-law's (Kornelius Kliewer's) mill in town was no longer standing. The Mennonite church in bad condition with the door standing open, the windows all without glass and boarded shut, empty inside but for the pigeons and starlings. The graveyard was worse, but some of the graves, including that of my grandmother's adoptive parents (Heinrich and Paulina Unruh) could still be made out.

On Sunday morning, the taxi arrived and the men drove to the nearby *Weichsel*, the Vistula, and parked by its banks, listening to the rush of water, and the wind through the strands of willow, the chirping of birds, then on through Wymysle Polski, the Polish settlement close by, where my grandfather saw, through the car window, someone he once knew. He did not state in the article who it was, and I wonder if he called out. What memories suddenly appeared? Had he smiled or felt regrets?

They returned to their village and Reinhold Wegert's house for a farewell lunch. At three o' clock they were picked up by car. The son-in-law of the owners of one of the other men's former family home would drive them. All this to say that the Polish residents went out of their way for these former residents who had come back to see the old home place.

The car drove away, slowly, so they could take in the village one last time. My grandfather admits he cried silently in the car.

From there they drove the eleven kilometers to Gabin, where Mr. Wegert's daughter lived. From there the men would be driven on to the train station in Kutno by taxi. When it was time to leave, my grandfather describes the men's surprise: "This dear friend from Gombin[4] had decorated his cab with flowers. This we didn't expect!"

Was this a simple gesture of peace between former German and Polish neighbors?

He had always gotten on well with his neighbors before the war, even during it, despite the dangerous climate. He never did get a chance to say his goodbyes to his homeplace on the day he was taken away. And while I don't recall my grandparents talking about the past, certainly not about the war, my aunt points out that yes, they did talk about the past. But they did not harbor bitterness, or dwell on bad memories. Those they had let go

---

4. The name of the town as it was known to my grandfather.

of. Still, perhaps by returning to Poland, my grandfather was able to find closure, even if he had not been seeking it.

~

At age eleven, in 1973, I was unaware of the complex person my grandfather was. I was living in a world that was still small, still in the shelter of family which, for all I could see, in ways I couldn't describe except that my grandparents weren't "from here," and despite a depth of dispossession I was still oblivious to, bore a silly similarity to the Clampetts of Beverly Hills. I was living a Canadian Mennonite life between worlds, where the only things I knew about prison camps were the slapstick escapades on my Opa's black-and-white TV.

There he is, my grandfather, on his fold-out chair in front of the television. I'm getting too old to sit on his lap, and besides, his stomach is so big I can only perch on his knees, but his arms beckon me. He still likes to bounce me on his knees, up and down. "Opa *schuckle* me," I begged of him when I was little. On screen in black and white, to the opening tune of banjos, Granny, Jed, Jethro, and Elly May, along with their doleful bloodhound, are driving in an old jalopy through palm tree- and mansion-lined streets. The picture slips vertically and there's a horizontal line through the screen, but it doesn't matter. I slide off his lap and adjust the rabbit ears a bit for Opa, then pull another stool up next to him. We are going to have a good time together this afternoon chuckling along with the laugh track.

10

Containers
(various definitions)

1. Objects used to hold something, especially when stored or transported.

2. Used to transport goods securely and efficiently from departure point to destination.

3. Plastic containers used to store food which became popular in the 1970s.

4. Self-contained (adj.); able to control one's feelings or emotions in the presence of others.

5. To contain something (verb); *a.* to have within, to hold; *b.* to comprise, to include; *c.* to enclose, to bind.

(from the O.E.D)

I.

My mother and her siblings—in their early seventies to late eighties—live within proximity of one another and gather frequently. Imagine all the birthdays; then throw in Christmas and summer gatherings, and Sunday afternoons, or weekday coffee klatches. I suppose that in the life of a former refugee immigrant family, gathering together is, in a sense, a way of keeping the family home. And despite a physical remove, the emotional bonds, or binds, remain.

Among her siblings, my mother often acquiesces to others' opinions, keeping her silence and wondering what the point would be of speaking her thoughts. No one seems to be listening. "You never say anything," one of the sisters chides her. She grew up the proverbial middle child, although technically that distinction would be her brother Bill's. In birth order, my mother is the seventh child of eleven that lived past their first year. I often wonder if all the children between the youngest and eldest in a large family aren't middle children. There has been much research done on birth order, though it's still considered the realm of pop psychology which posits the importance of birth order in determining character: the conscientiousness of the oldest child, the pampering of the youngest until the next child comes along. Alfred Adler, who died in 1937, a contemporary of Freud, was one of the first theorists to believe that birth order influences personality. Later, psychologists would argue that sibling personalities continue to develop throughout life, regardless of birth order.

When, not long ago, my mother's oldest sister Martha, older by a decade, was in the hospital with cancer, my mother brought her homemade *borscht*, still warm in the small container from home, and spooned it to her lips. I watched the two of them. They were quiet together, but for my mother asking, "How does it taste?"

"It's good," my aunt's reply.

II.

In the home in which I grew up, my mother stoically absorbed the strains of raising children, running a household, and helping my father in business. She told me her family home had always been a loud place. All those siblings, the noise, and the tension of old- and new-world values. She had wanted to leave. It was only natural, she said. At twenty, she was happy to marry my father, a young refugee and immigrant like her. She recognized in him the ambition for a new and better life.

Until she made a home with my father, my mother had lived in two different ones, each one in separate worlds, but in many temporary shelters along the way. The first home was the ancestral farmhouse in Poland, where the great room became the bedroom as table benches lined the wall for sleeping. The youngest children took turns sleeping in grandmother's bed, something they all wanted to do, because their aging widowed grandmother, their *Babtjche*, always had time for tenderness. But *Babtjche* died in 1943, when my mother, Erna, was four. During the war, the family was displaced, all the members scattered for a time, for years, until, together, they eventually crossed the border of Poland in the boxcar of a train. Not counting the years spent living in a refugee camp, in close quarters separated by blankets, or the year spent in Alberta working on a farm to pay off the travel debt, the next home was an improbably small farmhouse on ten acres of prairie in the Fraser Valley of British Columbia.

Erna and the younger three of her six sisters shared one bedroom and two beds, my grandparents the other bedroom, and the youngest boy, Bernie, had a place to sleep in something like a summer kitchen. I don't know if the next oldest brother, Bill, was still at home, but the older siblings—two brothers and two of the sisters—had all found jobs in Vancouver, married, and came home on weekends to help with seasonal chores; butchering, haying, picking crops, putting up the canning.

Even so, living at home was crowded, and so Erna was ready to leave. After she finished grade eleven—in the late 1950s that was enough education—she followed the path of her older siblings and moved to the city. She boarded with her next oldest sister, Emilie, compatible because Emilie, too, had a calm and peaceable nature.

My mother loved the city. The busyness of downtown was an external stimulant, not an internal anxiety; and exciting, nothing like the Mennonite communities—in the Polish village, in the refugee camp, or on the prairie—in which she'd been ensconced.

Such a rural life, where church and relatives and neighbors all run together like a thaw in spring, appears idyllic to those on the outside wishing for community. But to an insider, it can also be suffocating, though one would rarely admit this. It is the price of belonging. Neighbors watching the comings and goings of neighbors, tongues flapping like laundry in the breeze. Privacy and individuality are not virtues in the community. Even less so for immigrant families whose survival depend upon one another, and whose members help the group to re-establish itself.

Thus, in the city or at church, the young people from the same background, from the same villages, encountered one another and essentially kept their community while leaving the farm.

III.

There are certain ineradicable patterns stamped into our modern, first-generation Canadian lives. I grew up with a multitude of cousins and frequent family gatherings. I don't have a sister, but if I think of the closest relationship I have to a sister, I would say it is with two or three of my female cousins. Of my mother's sisters' daughters, Sharon was born the same year as me in 1962. She and I played together from infancy, in which we would have lain, swaddled, to nap side by side on a bed during family gatherings; we, the last of the post-Second-World-War baby-boomers. As teenagers in 1980, Sharon and I traveled to Europe together, red maple-leaf patches sewn to our back packs, sustaining ourselves with strong coffee, stale bread rolls, cheese, and chocolate. We still get together for coffee, dinner out, and a movie, or for the annual Mennonite Relief Sale held in late September in my hometown, where quilts, farm-grown produce, tables and bins of donated items, and bowls of *borscht* are sold by volunteers, former Mennonite refugees, and immigrants, raising vast sums for disaster relief and today's refugees.

The other night Sharon and I met for dinner. We were talking about her impending move. After taking a bite of salad, she asked me, "Do you save all your plastic shopping bags, too?" adding, "I have a drawer-full." I didn't view this as an odd question, or one coming out of nowhere. I laughed and thought of my own cupboard full of plastic bags, reusable but the quantity still mounting. Sharon and I made a verbal list of things we collect in our kitchens. Our drawers are filled with Ziploc bags we wash out to reuse; our cupboards are stacked with plastic cottage-cheese and yogurt tubs, ice cream buckets, milk bottles, and cartons. Containers.

"Maybe it has to do with the refugee experience," I said, and Sharon nodded. The reason was implicit to us both; in our DNA. Empty containers are not to be wasted. Containers, used for preserving and passing on something, symbolize the prospect of receiving. Having containers at the ready is a sign of abundance.

IV.

My mother and her sisters are a circle, impenetrable, it seems, even by daughters. At times I have felt that, while the relationship between my mother and me is loving and not argumentative, I cannot contend for, or partake of, the connection she shares with her sisters. Not that they demonstrate a particular intimacy. No; their bond is more like a cable, a steely fidelity formed by their shared childhoods and, perhaps uniquely, the particular traumas of war and their refugee-immigrant past.

My mother, a septuagenarian, has acquired the rare beauty of her age. I have always thought her attractive. With her lightened hair styled short, her understated taste in imported European clothing, she appears confident, though I know she has often felt overlooked. Growing up in a large family. Arriving in a new country at age thirteen with braids in her hair, learning English from a Grade One primary reader. Our experiences shape us.

For her seventy-fifth birthday, I wanted to do something I thought she would value, so I approached my aunts to arrange a gathering of just sisters, as they have always done in the past. Then I asked my mother, who dislikes surprises and being the focus of attention, to see if this would be all right. She reminded me that one younger sister would be away in Hawaii on the exact date, two other sisters no longer drive and the absent one is their designated driver, and another sister cannot leave her husband alone at home because his Alzheimer's has progressed. That would leave only the youngest sister.

Things are changing, my mother says. "Let's just you and I have lunch together."

Mother, daughter, sister, and friend, nest one inside the other, like a *matroyshka* doll.

V.

Do the river's bed and banks contain the river?

Does the firmament contain the stars?

What about the borders that divide land and countries, dividing the immigrant's present life from his or her past?

What, then, contains *us*? Is it our heritage? Our home? A place? Family?

Is our body the container of our DNA? Does our parents' DNA encode their past into our molecules of tissue, blood, and bone?

Do we contain memory? Or does Memory contain us?

What do we carry with us through life? And what do we leave when we die?

Does life *contain* paradox? Or is it paradox that *contains* life? The question may be phrased another way: Is paradox bound up in life, which is finite, or is paradox, without limits, the containment of life?

It seems to me that there is an amorphous relationship between the noun, that which contains, and the verb, *to contain*. The verb, the act of containing seems to seep *through* the noun—that which "encloses"—or overflow it. The noun, either finite or porous, the verb having the qualities of water.

It is life and paradox that overflow all confines, the way a flowing river is not contained by borders. Or how the sky is borderless. The universe expanding.

What is more, I have come to be comforted by the idea that it is in the nature of a question to grow, not to make small. Answers are a different matter. If this is so, questions are the crux of faith. And faith is expansive enough to hold doubt. This, again, is a paradox; the substance of life.

Like most people, I have been bound, enclosed, *and* upheld by culture, religion, heritage, and family. At times, I wrestle with this; at times, my cup overflows with its beneficence.

Repose

11

Oral History

(or, food-ways)

My memory has captured an image of her; apron-clad, in the kitchen, the table-top dusted with flour, her thick hands in dough and, as the table creaked under the weight of her efforts, my plump grandmother vigorously pummeling it so it would rise again, divine. Yet, as potent as an image is, and more than I might realize, memory is of the tongue.

~

In my grandmother's kitchen, the food of my childhood was not only delicious to the taste buds, but the foreign names, like *zwieback*[1]—the glide of vowels, diphthongs of dialect, and jumble of consonants in our mouths— were delectable to form in the palate. Others included *bobbat* (prune-and-raisin-studded dough baked in the cavity of a roast chicken), *kjielkje* (homemade noodles), and *plumi moos* (chilled plum soup). The meats, chicken or pork, were simply roasted or fried; my favorite: *kotletten* (meatballs) along with the tasty (and new-world) shake-n-bake chicken parts.

Meals were repetitive but never tedious. The aromas of the kitchen alternated between the sweetness of dough rising or bread baking, and savory soups—chicken noodle, aromatic from star anise and black peppercorns,

1. In German, all nouns, including names of food, are capitalized, but I have not done so.

thick with homemade ribbons of *kjielkje*, or cabbage *borscht*-flavored with bunches of dill, and in summertime, green or *sommer borscht* made from sorrel leaves with their distinctly sour taste, and buttermilk. The small kitchen warmed us with heat from the oven or stove, the front window streaked with steam, in summer, too, as *wareneki* (fruit or cottage cheese dumplings) boiled on the stovetop; these we ate with a sauce of butter and either sour or sweet cream. Summer was also the season for *rollkuchen* (deep fried dough rolled thin) fried to a crisp in oil and eaten with homemade damson plum or apricot jam, or slices of chilled watermelon. *Rollkuchen* with watermelon constituted many a summer meal, the ripe melons bought from the truck in the parking lot at the Food Liner or at Funk's Super Market. The town's two Mennonite grocers were situated kitty-corner from one another at the intersection of the main road, South Fraser Way, and Clearbrook Road, the road from the highway leading into Clearbrook, our town.

With the exception of a Chinese restaurant and the *A&W* drive-in, most of the businesses along the main road through town were owned by Mennonites: the Texaco gas station, Clearbrook Hardware, the Bible book store, the light fixture store, the doctor, and dentist. But in the 1960s and early 1970s, we Mennonite families ate at home, and the equivalent of a night out was dinner at Oma's.

And women wanted to know of their husbands, whose *borscht* tasted better, whose *rollkuchen* crisper—your mother's or mine? My father's high praise sounded like this, "This tastes as good as my mother used to make."

Mennonite food. That's what we called it. The recipes were imprinted in the mind of my grandmother, who made everything from memory, passed down by her mother (an aunt, actually, who raised her as her own). My acculturating mother, too, roasted Sunday noon meals of chicken and *bobbat*, cooked *borscht*, boiled *wareneki*, baked *paska* every Easter, fried *rollkuchen* in summer and conserved plum jam, and deep-fried *porzelkie* (raisin fritters) at New Year's.

My mother would have learned from her mother, and also from *The Mennonite Treasury of Recipes* on our kitchen shelf; in 1961, the year before I was born, a group of women from Steinbach, a Mennonite enclave in Manitoba, collected these traditional recipes into a book. My grandmother gave me a copy for my wedding shower in 1982, when I was twenty. Like a good Mennonite wife in the new world, I would, she assumed, bake, boil, and fry dough for my husband and children like the frugal Mennonite women of the Old World in Poland and Russia in the years of farming and famine; create from it our sustenance, preserve our heritage, and thus, our identity.

Perhaps most "Mennonite" of all, my mother, baked buns on Saturdays. And as anyone in the Mennonite circle knows, *zwieback* is as substantive to the Mennonite family as bread is to communion.

On the backside of the introductory page in the yellowed copy of my *Mennonite Treasury of Recipes*, which lost its soft cover years ago but is still bound together by a coil, the "committee," as the three women called themselves, going by the names of their husbands, Mrs. Peter Rosenfeld, Mrs. D.D. Warkentin and Mrs. Jac. H. Peters, had this to say under the heading *Wheat, Mennonites, and Zwieback*:

> *Wherever our people settled, they grew wheat. No wonder our mothers and grandmothers were experts baking breads and Zwieback. No one had to go hungry as long as there was bread in the house, and where can you find a more delicious aroma than stepping into a Low German Mennonite home on a Saturday afternoon where freshly baked buns are taken out of the oven?*[2]

My mother baked on Saturdays, and my parents held to the tradition of Sunday *faspa*, an evening meal of bread and cheese, perhaps sliced meats, some canned pickles.

> *Sunday "Faspa" when visitors came, Tweback [Zwieback] were always served with coffee. Some prefer to dunk them, others believe dunking spoils the taste. Butter was never served with the buns as the goodness of butter was already baked in the buns.*[3]

It was also the meal served at weddings. On my mother's wedding day, she helped my grandmother bake the *zwieback* for the wedding meal; relatives, friends, all the people of the Mennonite congregation, three hundred or more in total, were invited and ate in shifts at folding tables in the church basement.

This simple meal was also the meal of funerals and often still is today for those who wish to keep with tradition and nostalgia, holding ritual in Mennonite Church basements, and then in church gyms when they were added. And I admit, *zwieback* seems fitting for a memorial service; to "eat this in remembrance." When my grandmother passed away in 1999, after

---

2. Steinbach Committee, *Mennonite Treasury*, 2.

3. Ibid., 2.

her funeral service we ate a *faspa* of buns and cheese in the basement of the Mennonite Brethren Church where she had been a devoted member.

In many ways, *zwieback* is a comfort food.

Typically, *zwieback* is the twice-baked bread enriched with egg and milk that small children eat. In Dutch, these slices are called *rusks* and differ from the version of *zwieback* I know, or *Tweebak* as the women in the *Mennonite Treasury of Recipes* call it in the Low German dialect (with capitalized nouns), those egg- and milk-enriched yeast double buns made from two balls of dough, one larger on the bottom, and one smaller pinch of dough on top.

I also think of how, during the war, the Mennonite mothers in Russia, Ukraine, and Poland prepared *zwieback* in preparation for fleeing the frontlines and armies. This *zwieback* would also have been twice baked, or roasted and dried, rather than double stacked, provisions for the journey over the weeks and months in the boxcars crammed with refugees, or on the horse-drawn wagon-trains attempting to escape the tanks and bombers.

The *zwieback* baked on Saturdays for Sunday *faspa*, eaten at wedding banquets and funerals, are deliciously sweet and soft "double buns" formed from two pieces of dough on top of one another, and pulled apart when eaten—the bottom bun with its small well perfect for a dollop of jam or, for those who defied convention, a melting pat of butter. My mother didn't bother with two balls of dough but she would have remained true to the recipe in the *Mennonite Treasury of Recipes,* which stated, "add enough flour to make a stiff dough." However much flour that was could only be learned through experience.

~

Marlene Epp, a Canadian scholar and historian, has written about the role of foods in Mennonite identity and states that "foodways" plays a key role in creating a community identity.[4] Foodways, she explains, were often the site at which the old and new worlds met.[5] While Mennonites claim their own gastronomy in Mennonite cookbooks, and food may be one of the last remaining ties to ancestral cultural tradition, and while Russia, Ukraine, and Poland are ancestral homelands, conversely it can be said that the early separatist Mennonites (Swiss, German, Dutch, Prussian) were more religiously than ethnically distinct—albeit belief certainly shapes

4. Epp, "More Than Just Recipes," 182.

5. Ibid., 174, 182.

culture—and foods, like the Mennonites themselves, migrated into homes and onto tables *from* the kitchens of Russia, Ukraine, and Poland.

Indeed, *zwieback* may have had its origins in sixteenth-century Netherlands, dating back to the time of the Reformation and Menno Simons. Although this is speculation drawn from the name of a street, "*Tweebak-markt*" (*Zwieback* Market).[6]

In 2005, during a trip to Moscow, in a journal entry about a visit to the Tretyakov Gallery, I noted what I had for lunch in a Russian restaurant across the street from the gallery: familiar food, *borscht*, meat-filled pastries (*pirozhki*) and meat–filled dumplings (*pilmenje*), like those I had stuffed myself with when I visited my father's Russian Mennonite cousins in Germany. They had emigrated from the Soviet Union in the 1970s, when Germany resettled those whose Prussian ancestors had migrated to Russia and later suffered oppression under the Communist regime. My own family did not cook *pilmenje* at home, we ate the meatless *vereniki* (*wareneki*), cottage cheese and fruit-filled dumplings, which originated in Ukraine. The *pilmenje* were eaten in the Siberian region in which Mennonites also established colonies, and the delectable meat dumplings may have come to Russia from China when trade routes were established.[7]

It also occurs to me that perhaps in that Russian restaurant there was as much history and story in the food on my tongue as in the paintings of the Russian masters and the Soviet artists hanging in the gallery.

And here I must mention the slices of Ukrainian watermelon we ate outdoors in the garden of a woman in my father's former childhood village when we visited her on that trip in 2005. The woman's family resettled in the village on the steppes in 1946 and occupied the houses after the villagers—"German" like my father's family—had been evacuated by the German army. The Mennonites call watermelon *harbuz* or *arbuz,* from the Russian word *arbus*, the name and the fruit adopted from Turkey. Those watermelons, my father always told us when we were children, were the sweetest ones, his childhood watermelons *even better* than the ones that would form our childhood memories.

There, in my father's former village, we figuratively, if not literally, broke bread together, but before we all partook, the Ukrainian woman handed my father the center piece of the watermelon, the *obraumtje* as he,

---

6. Ibid., 181. Also Voth Jost, *Mennonite Food and Folkways*, Vol. I, 36.

7. Voth Jost, *Mennonite Food and Folkways*, Vol. I, 194.

a boy on the steppes, would have called it in Low German—this piece of significance with its own name, a word to roll the tongue around.

Later, my father told us it wasn't as sweet as he remembered.

⌒

What is interesting to me now is how instantly taste transports us geographically, temporally. Our histories, our roots, and our food are inextricably linked. The food in our mouths, the taste on our tongues, engender a narrative of our past.

Anne Applebaum, the Warsaw correspondent for the *Washington Post*, winner of the Pulitzer Prize for non-fiction in 2004 for her book, *Gulag: A History*, has also written *Iron Curtain, The Crushing of Eastern Europe, 1944–1956*. Her work interests me in large part because of my family history in both Ukraine and Poland; it is a contested history wherein personal stories unfold only long after the public narratives of the War in Europe, the Holocaust, are over, and *after* the collapse of the Soviet Union. Who could talk about the war and the suffering of Mennonites and Germans under the weight of the Jewish experience? Who could talk about life under the Communist regime until the threat of danger to loved ones left behind was past?

Gulag is the history of the Soviet concentration camps in the Gulag Archipelago that had their origins in the Bolshevik Revolution and developed into a major part of the Soviet economy. My paternal grandparents and father lived through these times. I turned to this book as a resource when I researched and tried to understand my father's family history in Stalinist Russia in order to write about it.

Writing about the camps—which were built for non-criminal civilian prisoners, a people deemed the "enemy," in order to dehumanize, persecute, and destroy them on a mass scale—Applebaum covers the origins, life, and work in the Soviet camps as an industrial complex. She sets out to show how the Gulag system and the Nazi system were founded on the same principles held by dictators who knew of one another's ideologies.

In her epilogue, "Memory," she writes:

> Half a century after the war's end, the Germans still conduct regular public disputes about victim's compensations, about memorials, about new interpretation of Nazi history. . . . Half a century after Stalin's death, there were no equivalent arguments taking

place in Russia, because the memory of the past was not a living part of public discourse.[8]

In *Iron Curtain,* Applebaum offers insights into the silences in my mother's family's experience in Poland. She writes about the expulsions of Germans at the close of the war. Many people categorized as *Volksdeutsch,* she writes in her chapter "Ethnic Cleansing," signed lists identifying themselves as such, for various reasons. For some it was ethnic pride, and for others the motive was fear of arrest and forced labor, or a desire for better treatment. In Poland in November 1946, the security police authorized roundups and forced those identified as ethnically German into labor camps, sometimes in former Nazi concentration camps.[9] The resettling of the German populations of Eastern Europe at the close of the war was an

> extraordinary mass movement, probably unequalled in European history. By the end of 1947, some 7.6 million Germans—including ethnic Germans, *Volksdeutsche* and recent settlers—had left Poland, through transfer or escape. About 400,000 died from hunger or disease on the way back to Germany or because they were caught in the crossfire of the advancing front.[10]

Historian Modris Eksteins writes that throughout Central and Eastern Europe, twelve to fifteen million Germans were expelled, encountering allied atrocities as German cities were carpet-bombed. Millions endured Soviet brutality during the advance of the Red Army. Two million did not survive.[11] The numbers are so dumbfounding that it's only in the stories, in the barest words and between the lines, that I can see my own mother as a child, her siblings and parents, the people of her village in flight.

∿

Perhaps it should not be a surprise to me that Anne Applebaum, so invested in the history of Eastern Europe, of Poland, where she lives part of the time, also co-authored a cookbook, *From a Polish Country Kitchen House,* after her husband's family purchased a Polish manor in 1989. After Communism was dismantled, they restored the house and began to cook. And yet, I was surprised by a simple recipe I found in its pages for *mizeria,*

8. Applebaum, *Gulag,* 569.

9. Ibid., 121.

10. Applebaum, *Iron Curtain,* 123.

11. Eksteins, *Walking Since Daybreak,* 215.

or Polish cucumber salad: 2 cucumbers, seeded, 1tsp. sugar, 1 tbsp. chopped fresh dill, 2 tbsp. white wine vinegar, salt, and freshly grated pepper. The recipe leaves out the cream, but notes this is how it is usually served. Just as my grandmother had done, although she used regular white vinegar. As a child in my maternal grandmother's kitchen, my favorite accompaniment to her food was this cucumber salad! How could cucumbers taste so good? She served this salad with *kotletten* (meatballs) and yellow fleshed potatoes from her garden, boiled, with butter and salt—potatoes we children called Polish potatoes—for what other potatoes would our grandmother from Poland cook? Recorded evidence of the past lived by my parents and grandparents; in this case, not historical research, writing, or story, but an alphabet of tastes remembered, of something from Poland that my Mennonite grandmother brought to the table.

Or, with respect to some of the food, it was the other way around. As Applebaum explains, Poles have always had a fondness for imported queens and foreign monarchs. Foreign influences, including Russian, German, Swedish, French, Italian, and Hungarian, can be found in Polish cooking and culture, so that it is hard to say where Polish food ends and where Russian and Ukrainian influences begin. This is evident in my *Mennonite Treasury of Recipes.*

⁓

On the family trip to Europe in 2005 when we visited my father's village on the Ukrainian steppes, we had also visited my mother's rural village in Poland. I was amazed by the mushrooms growing in the field that was the site of her childhood home. They were the size of dinner plates! I know next to nothing about mushrooms, but I do know that foraging for them in the forest is a family tradition in Poland. However, mushrooms are not part of Mennonite cookery. Were these mothers and cooks uncertain as to which mushrooms were poisonous? Or perhaps these people simply preferred pork and meat to the earthy flesh of fungi, actually a fruit body. Nevertheless, what remains almost tangible about that August afternoon visit to my mother's former Mennonite village is not only the images of the fields, the old home sites—or even the strand of wildflowers preserved in my journal—but the experience of tasting freshly picked mushrooms simmered in broth.

As our driver pulled the van to a dusty stop and parked at the entrance to the quiet farming village, a local Polish woman in a polka-dotted dress greeted us. We learned she had lived there since 1947; her family had been resettled in the village after the German occupation, after the majority of the village residents fled in advance of the Russian troops. This woman would have been born around the time of my grandmother's departure as a refugee with her children.

"You must stop by my house before you leave," she said to us.

We spent the late morning and early afternoon walking the sand road past the farms. Some of the houses from my mother's childhood still remained, though hers was gone. While much had changed with time and neglect—the Mennonite church had begun to crumble from disuse, the old cemetery was overgrown—in some ways, time had seemed to stop. The farming was mostly managed without machinery, the hay was uncut. In the heat, the abiding low humming of grasshoppers and bees.

This lazy afternoon a group of teenage boys gathered along fence posts, curious about us as we walked down the lane of their hometown. I suspect other residents—reticent or occupied with laundry, housekeeping, or barn chores, but curious—watched us through curtains as we passed their yards. But, no doubt, this woman in the polka-dotted dress knew a business opportunity when she saw one in the form of foreigners arriving to visit their old homestead.

As we concluded our visit and returned to our van, she was waiting and beckoned us to a mid-day meal she had prepared for us. "Just pay me what you can," she said. (Afterward, I saw as my father slipped her a hundred-dollar bill.)

Who could refuse? The seven of us—my parents, my husband and me, our two teenage sons and our twenty-year-old daughter—along with our driver, gathered around a wooden table set up in her back yard, where around and beneath it the chickens scrabbled for insects, and close by, inside her yard, the teenage boys lined her fence like a row of sunflowers to watch. Hungry, perhaps; gazing at the beautiful girl from Canada, with her long blonde hair, eating lunch in the sunlight.

The woman explained to us that after we arrived and while we were out walking she had gathered mushrooms in the forest and cooked a soup. She served us glasses of cold cherry juice made from cherries from the tree and the well in the yard, and a first course of mushroom broth ladled over noodles. Noodles, like the *kjielkje* my grandmother would have made in her kitchen, in this village, just down the road. From flour, milk, and eggs, and when the hens were laying well, made in large quantity, then dried and always on hand just as the cookbook, *Mennonite Foods and Folkways*, describes.

After a deep bowlful of hearty soup, the woman served us a second course of homemade unpasteurized cottage cheese with fresh cream, hoisting her massive bowl, liberally shoveling cheese into our basin-like emptied ones, one by one, and when she came to me, and I asked for only a little, like a specter of my grandmother who thought a small appetite meant that her food wasn't tasty, the woman filled my bowl, stood over me and watched to ensure I ate it all.

～

When my husband and I returned to Poland in May 2013, en route from Berlin to Warsaw, we shared a rail compartment with a Polish graduate student, a research biologist in immunology who was traveling with her small daughter. On the course of our journey together with the young woman, who had just visited with her parents in the countryside, we engaged in a conversation about food. Specifically, on the subject of *barszcz* (*borscht*). Her mother cooked beet *barszcz*, she said; our mothers cooked cabbage and meat *borscht*. "You must try *zurek*—white *barszcz*," she said, "it is special to Poland." It was her favorite.

It must be like summer *borscht*, a soup I love, with its sour and creamy base, served with a boiled egg in each bowl. *Sommer borscht*—"Mennonite Soup" it is called, according to a recipe in my *Mennonite Treasury of Recipes*

"Does it have sorrel in it to give it the sour flavor?" I asked the young woman.

No, the woman said, this soup is made with a base of *zakwas*—rye flour or bread and water, like a sourdough starter. The stock of this hearty vegetable and sausage soup is sour, salty, and creamy, although it too, like *sommer borscht*, is served with a boiled egg in it.

My husband and I sampled various versions of *borscht* all throughout the city of Krakow. And while I did not find *sommer borscht*, and *zakwas* was delicious, I felt gratified when I later discovered, in the pages of Applebaum and Crittenden's *From a Polish Country House Kitchen*, a recipe for *zupa szczawiowa*, sorrel soup, complete with directions to garnish with a hardboiled egg, preferably a quail's egg, for added protein.

Applebaum says in Poland's restaurants there is a return to simple foods. True. From Krakow's fine dining and more rustic establishments we also sampled *pierogi*, or what we had called *wareneki* at home. We ate *pierogi* filled with cherries, served with butter and cream. My favorite summer meal as a child, the main and only course, not served as dessert on china, eaten with silver cutlery, as I now enjoyed them.

~

I remember one summer camping trip in Penticton, British Columbia, with relatives on my mother's side. In the heat of one July afternoon in the late 1960s, on the picnic tables in front of the campers and tents, the women prepared *wareneki*, Aunt Elsie, my mother's energetic cousin from Alberta, leading the charge. There, my mother and aunts pitting ice-cream pails full of fresh Okanagan cherries, rolling out dough with the rolling pins they'd brought camping, cutting out rounds of dough by pressing the mouths of coffee mugs into it, folding these rounds over the fruit to form the dumplings, and boiling potful after potful on Coleman stoves. A laborious effort for their hungry husbands and children after a day at the beach. We ate them as fast as they made them.

Wareneki, along with *rollkuchen* and watermelon, or thin rolled pancakes (named German pancakes in the *Treasury*) with fresh peaches and whipped cream, or simply with plum, cherry, or apricot jam, were summer meals in Mennonite families. These were the childhood feasts our mothers made with flour, the recipes from a time in history when there was little to eat but what one grew from the earth. *Mehl speise*, the Mennonites called this, roughly translated as meals from flour. "Many of these meals hail back from the days of want and austerity, and are no longer in use, but may be of interest for coming generations to read," the women of Steinbach, Manitoba wrote in 1961 in the introduction to their cookbook. Fifty years later the recipes are of interest to me, and the memories are still as fresh as summer fruit.

A more recent summer memory is breakfast on the deck at our lake house. My parents had arrived by boat from their summer residence across the water, my mother bearing gifts, jars of freshly made cherry and apricot jam, just picked and preserved from the fruit trees in her yard. My grown children were visiting for the long weekend. It was Saturday morning, and my husband was making thin pancakes, what you might call crepes.

We both grew up eating these rolled pancakes with jam. Filled with cottage cheese, their name becomes *blintze*. They are *flinsen* or *pflinzen* in Low German, or simply, Dutch or German pancakes in the *Treasury* cookbook. *Nalesniki* in Polish, "the thing you make when there is nothing in the house but eggs and flour," it says in *From a Polish Country House Kitchen*. It occurs to me that *this* simple meal, pancakes, if not *zwieback*, is the fullest trace of my Mennonite ancestry, its' origins in the Reformation in Switzerland, and in the Netherlands where a converted priest's—Menno Simon's—Protestant Pacifist sect formed. From here, the pathway of its migration on to the Vistula Delta, embracing a Prussian German identity under Frederick the Great who offered religious freedom and land to farm in an area that would later again become Poland. In time, Catherine the Great of Russia (formerly a German princess) invited the Mennonites to form colonies on land she had gained in the Ukraine region (from the Turks).

I can visualize my husband standing at the stove with my son-in-law, who is of Swiss and Italian ancestry, showing him how to make these thin pancakes—a breakfast tradition in our home—a slab of butter melting in the frying pan. My husband pouring the batter into the pan, swirling it to make a thin layer, his pancakes nice and thin while his protégé's pancakes thicken with inexperience.

⁓

Saturday morning pancakes. We each have our own memories associated with food and ritual. In eating these foods I am reminded of *who* I come from, the people before me. Food imparts the flavor of belonging. As I think of the food my grandmother cooked, I see more clearly, the older I get, that she had preserved something of her past, and of another place, indelibly connecting me to each, and to her. Food is our family story, but a story without words. It is the language my grandmother spoke, but without speech.

After the bowl of batter was scraped clean, the last pancake browned, and the plate piled with them, we all gathered around the table on the deck, the lake below us, my parents, our son and his fiancé, my daughter, her husband (our youngest son and his girlfriend, absent). But before we could eat, our daughter and son-in-law wanted to show something to their grandparents, something they had shared with the rest of us the night before. My daughter passed a rolled up paper to my mother, who unfurled it, and stared, at first not fully comprehending the image—vague but distinguishable and recognizable, not unlike memory. But not of the past, rather, an ultrasound image of the future! And with that, while I no longer was the one doing all the cooking, I was on the way to becoming the grandmother in the kitchen.

12

Pilgrimage

I.

Place is as evocative, perhaps as intimate as memory, to one like me who has never before been to these former Mennonite villages in Poland's Vistula Delta. The fields of yellow rapeseed, flax in shades of blue, purple alfalfa, and rye, bloom brightly among the silvered fields of barley and wheat, and patches of cornstalks, potatoes, sugar beets, and ripening strawberries. Old houses are clad with age-blackened and silvered planks, shutters painted green and gold, lace curtains in windows. Blue delphiniums and pink geraniums grow in flower gardens and wild poppies fringe the fields, or sometimes form a whole blanket of vibrant red. The red brick barns signify former Mennonite farms, the stork's nests like giant straw hats on top of poles or old chimneys. Here, budding open in the late spring, is every shade of green—birch, chestnut, pine, poplar, willow, the mountain ash in June before the berries brighten to orange, and rows of linden trees, their verdant canopies lining the country roads, planted centuries ago to provide shade or a break from the wind as the Mennonites' horses and wagons traveled along them.

We see the lindens from a distance. In some areas there isn't a former Mennonite house or barn nearby, only the boundless fields, tracts of land that have transitioned from Soviet collectives post-1945 to present-day free-market farming co-operatives. In places where villages no longer stand, the lindens are the only reminder. And all throughout is the spine of dike alongside the river, the signature of the Mennonite's labor that created this landscape from the river's marshland.

I have come here once more with my mother and father, traveling together with them as I have done before to Poland and to Ukraine in 2005. This time we have joined a group comprised of other Mennonites, from British Columbia, Manitoba, Ontario, California and Nebraska. Alan, the Executive Director of the Mennonite Historical Society of California has organized this geographical and genealogical journey aptly called, "Mennonites in Poland." Along narrow country roads, conspicuous in our tour bus, and foreign, we seek the remnants of a family heritage once grounded in the Mennonites of Danzig/Gdansk.[1] We retrace our migrations from Gdansk, up-river, against the current, away from the sea.

~

Pilgrimage: a journey to a place of connection to the sacred. For Catholics and Protestants, the most popular are the Holy Land and Jerusalem; Rome; the path of the broken heart to our Lady of Guadalupe in Mexico City; the Camino trail, otherwise known as the Way of Saint James, across Spain to the relics of the apostle in the Cathedral of Santiago de Comp Estela. A pilgrimage is also a journey to a place that has, to them, a moral or spiritual significance. So perhaps I might use the term pilgrimage, albeit loosely, to describe my return to Poland in June 2014, for my third time, to specifically explore the places and sites where my ancestors, on the heels of the Protestant Reformation sweeping through Europe, founded their villages and churches. But I am a traveler, a tourist, and not as diligent on my spiritual path as I might be.

The solid bones, beam and brick, of former Mennonite churches still dot the Polish countryside. In some rural villages, stone foundations reveal the outline of a vanished church and congregation. In a former time, up until my grandparents' middle age, and when my own parents were young children, Mennonite life and society was built on the firm foundation of the church. Churches kept records of births and deaths, baptisms, marriages, and thus, lineages. The church and its congregation were central to one's identity and belonging.

---

1. The names of cities are given in German as they were known in Prussia, followed by their current and Polish names.

This Protestant offshoot I stem from was named after its founder, Menno Simons, a former Catholic priest who joined the Anabaptists in 1536. Mennonites were a sect of this heretical movement, and they, along with other Anabaptist sects, were persecuted during the Reformation in central Europe, and in the Inquisition that spread to the Netherlands, for having converted from Catholicism. Mennonites believed in the separation of Church and State, the practice of adult baptism, pacifism, and its stance of conscientious objection to war. They were known particularly for their passive resistance to violence, and for some, non-resistance to violence. Persecuted as they were, they venerated the idea of identifying with Christ through suffering and death.

For Mennonites, the holiest book after the Bible is *Martyrs Mirror*—the full title is *The Bloody Theater or Martyrs Mirror of the Defenseless Christians who baptized only upon confession of faith, and who suffered and died for the testimony of Jesus, their Savior, from the time of Christ to the year A.D. 1660* (the word *defenseless* refers to the Anabaptist belief in non-resistance). The book, complete with ink etchings, is filled with stories of tongue screws and burning pyres to silence the prayers and proclamations of the faithful new Protestants, as well as drownings in the river—believers bound with rope and weighted down with a sack of rocks for good measure. First published in Holland in 1660, in Dutch, by Thieleman J. van Braght, the tome documents the stories and testimonies of Christian martyrs over seventeen centuries, up to and including the Anabaptists and, consequently, Mennonites.

Later, suffering was the trope in the stories of Mennonites who, after three hundred years, migrated away from Poland and experienced Revolution in the Russian Empire, and then Stalin's purges in the Soviet Union soon after. Exile for five and ten years of hard labor. Round-ups and mass arrests. My paternal grandfather was a Mennonite pastor silenced under a Communist regime, but that story, set in Ukraine, I have written elsewhere.[2]

⁓

When we arrived in Poland, Alan handed out copies of the genealogical research he prepared. Now as we meander the country roads, he points out the areas where an ancestor lived. He has traced each of our lineages back to these farmlands, and my father, who was born in Ukraine, is for the first time, connected to the same country as my mother who lived in

2. *The Steppes are the Color of Sepia: A Mennonite Memoir.*

Poland until late 1948. "We came from Prussia," my father has said. For the first time, at eighty-three, he sees, as do I, this land, in Poland, that was once the Prussia of his family line. The city of Gdansk itself was built on land that had been part of Poland since 1308, until the first partition in 1772 when it became part of Prussia. Gdansk remained a free state until the second partition in 1793, when it, too, became Prussian.

The earliest known Mennonite ancestor on my father's side died in 1757, according to church records, but his date of birth is unknown so it might be assumed that he was born shortly after the time of *Martyrs'* publication. His name was Jacob Letkemann. He was born beyond the environs of Gdansk, in the village of Altendorf, on farmland below sea-level created by dikes. Jacob was from a family of original German settlers to the Vistula delta, and may have joined the Anabaptist Mennonites as an adult and been baptized sometime in the 1700s. This may explain why there is no recorded date of birth.

My mother's side reaches further back, to the bustling seaport and trade city, to the last decades of the sixteenth century. Her genealogy reveals an accumulation of descendants from Switzerland, Moravia, Hungary, joining the Mennonite fold, among those who migrated to the lowlands of Friesland, and on to the Kingdom of Poland where people did not have to assume the belief of their sovereign.

In Gdansk in the 1500s, the Mennonites enjoyed religious freedom, but as pacifists they could not be citizens, nor own land, nor belong to a trade guild, and were not permitted to construct church buildings in the city. Eventually, they were not permitted to live within the walls of the city, although there is a house, tall and thin with Dutch Renaissance lines, on beautiful Mariacka Street, *Ano 1704* still visibly inscribed on it. For a time after it was built, it served as a Mennonite house of worship. What piques my interest is that next door to the Mennonite "church" had lived Schopenhauer's mother.

The philosopher Schopenhauer was born in Gdansk. He viewed the world as a place of endless strife, believing that transcendence of the human condition may be sought through asceticism, moral awareness, and aesthetic perception. In certain ways, Mennonites believed in asceticism with their simple lifestyle, and held to a moral awareness in their piety, but their own churches were without adornments. Sculpture or art of any sort would be considered idolatry.

But this is not to say that Mennonites were not artists. Gdansk bears the traces of Abraham van den Blocke, a Flemish architect and sculptor who came to the city in the mid-1500s, and of his brothers Isaac, Jacob, and David—Mennonites, all master painters and craftsmen, who left their imprint (and graven images) on St. Mary's Cathedral (said to be the largest brick church in the world), the Town Hall ceilings, and throughout the city. Abraham is most known for his construction of Gdansk's city gate, the "Golden Gate," built in 1612 and completed in 1614.

Our group wanders through the historic sites and the Golden Gate. Outside the gate, beyond the outskirts of the old city's limits, we can see it. A large church, its plaster the shade of butter cream, within walking distance of where we stand even though we climb aboard the waiting tour bus so we don't have to walk along, or cross, the busy traffic arteries of the sprawling city. Like the tourists we are, we are driven the short distance to the former Mennonite church. Built in 1808, its congregation originally formed after a union of the Old Flemish Mennonite congregation (founded in 1569) and the Old Frisian Mennonite congregation (founded about 1600) and after both their church buildings had been destroyed in the Napoleonic Wars. The street leading to the church still bears the name *Mennonicki Uli.*

With the fall of Communism, this modest yet capacious and persistent structure, luminous against the hill, once again serves as a Protestant church. Beside it is the brick building that was formerly a hospice in keeping with the custom of the Mennonite congregation to provide care to the sick, elderly, and poor. I pause outside as the others go in. I notice the pockmarks in the brick building, in the plaster of the church, a reminder of the war, and of the resilience of not merely the buildings but of the spirit of people who have occupied them, then and now.

I don't know if my ancestors had ever attended here. Records state that my father's great-great-grandfather, Heinrich Peter Letkemann, was born in Tiegenhagen, a distance away. But he may have migrated to South Russia as early as 1803 before the church was built, though other migration records state 1818,[3] so there is a possibility he had come here, this being the mother church of all the smaller surrounding congregations.

∿

Prior to emigrating to Russia, my father's forbearers migrated south from Gdansk, down the Vistula river's course to the drained farmland

---

3. Schapansky, "The Early Letkemanns," 2.

below, referred to as the *grosses* (big) *Werder*—the triangle of land that lies between the Nogat and Vistula rivers and the Baltic Sea. These people were religious, and they worked hard—an attribute maintained to this day, as if by a dike along bloodlines. Some ancestors also settled in the city of Elbing/Elblag, or further south along the river, in the lowlands at Marienburg/Marbork at the foot of the Teutonic Knight's massive red brick castle. How surprised my husband and I were to learn that both his and my ancestors had lived in Marienburg, to realize that not until hundreds of years later, after our parents immigrated to Canada, to British Columbia, to the Fraser River's valley in the aftermath of World War II, would our two families reside once again in the same town! And we two would marry.

As part of the agreement with their Sovereign, King Frederick III, the Mennonites of Poland made payments to the government to ensure that their sons would not have to serve in the military. Nonetheless, my father's family, as did the ancestors of my husband, remained in the Vistula delta only until Catherine the Great, royalty of Prussia, invited the Mennonites to farm the steppes of southern Russia (what would become Ukraine). Their industrious reputation was known to the Czarina; they had drained the Vistula's marshland just as they had done before in Holland—with a system of dikes along the river that today still hold back the river. It seems the Russian Czarina was presenting a better offer—not only freedom of religion but free land and *free* exemption from military service. My father's Mennonites were among those who set off with horse and wagon for Ukraine. The Mennonites who remained in Prussia were generally established, owning estates, which they were not permitted to sell. Either they could afford the payments, *or* they no longer subscribed to pacifism which had once been a tenet of their faith. Or, in some cases both: money and a less conservative view of war was the reason for staying.

~

On this beautiful summer day, on a narrow country road, we arrive at a cemetery in the village of Syznich, not far from the city of Kulm/Chelmno, a burial place where some of us may find the gravesite of an ancestor. The stone markers are on a grassy hillside. As I look back towards the country road, I see a man with a walking stick and cap coming along the way. An image so like the memory of my own grandfather Schroeder who has been dead for more than three decades.

We are here to see the tombstone of a Mennonite leader, Abraham Nickel, who made the contract with King Frederick III (who succeeded to the throne in 1797) to pay 30,000 *thaler* (almost 500,000 *euros* today, my husband calculates) to the widows and children of soldiers, plus 5,000 *thaler* per year so Mennonite boys would not have to fight in the army. It is still preserved in this former Mennonite cemetery of the Schönsee congregation, which now belongs to a Catholic church in Szynych. Nickel was originally buried in a Mennonite cemetery in nearby Schönsee, or Sosnowka as it is called in Polish today. From that overgrown site, his marker was brought to this tended-to cemetery on a rolling field and tree-filled hillside. His is the large black granite stone that, in a sardonic twist, bears bullet holes from a skirmish during the Second World War.

Here, on a small knoll among pine trees and high grass, where other stones still remain, I come across the name David Schroeder (1843–1917). He is not, of course, my mother's teenage brother (David Schroeder, 1925–1943) killed in action in World War II in Ukraine and buried in an unmarked grave. Even so, among the pines and broken remains, located near a vanished Mennonite village in Poland, his same name is etched in stone.

~

My mother's ancestors migrated from the north, following the Vistula River, some settling in villages throughout the *Werder* or the city of Kulm/ Chelmno, and further along to the southernmost point of Mennonite settlements of Kazun and Czermno, in an area approximately 100 kilometers from Warsaw. Here, by 1750, my mother's line was rooted, although other extended family members migrated to Russia in the latter part of the eighteenth century, as well as to the United States and Canada in the early part of the twentieth.

Nevertheless, here in Poland's lowlands near Warsaw, my mother was born, and her family remained in Poland in the village Deutsch Wymyschle now named Novo Wymysle with its Polish spelling—she, her mother and youngest siblings—until 1948. The heritage signs in former Mennonite villages erected by the local Polish governments and the European Union announce that "*these Mennonites from the Netherlands lived in the Vistula Delta from CA 1540 to 1945.*" There are no known Mennonites living in Poland today, guides, scholars, and historians all state. Within that official phrase an implicit complex history has run through my story like the river Vistula that begins and ends in Poland, its wide silver band flanked by white sandy beaches and willows, its shimmer concealing eddies, currents, and undertow.

Pilgrimage as a journey to a place of connection. This aspect of returning once more to Poland becomes real for me. It is astonishing to me how land, how touching down on it, walking and driving through it, the roads, the rolling fields of the *Werder* (*Zulawy* in Polish) and the dikes alongside the river, can give me such a connection to the past. It is as if, through place, time's dimension dissipates. The towns and cities may have changed, but despite reconstructed squares and centers, as is the case throughout Poland, I can go back to the site of childhood (my mother's), or even before that, as I have, to the site of both my paternal and maternal ancestors where I can see the traces of their presence.

II.

The Vistula is the river's name in Latin. It is *Wisla* in Polish. It is the *Weichsel* in my Mennonite ancestor's German language. The wide river undulates like cursive script across a page. Place is what connects me to my story, and to a time before memory; a connection ineffable, intimate, and perhaps sacred.

The river begins in Poland's Carpathian and Tetra mountains and, flowing north, runs through the hills and delta and ends in Gdansk, where it pours itself into the Baltic Sea. This river is my bloodline through the land; the land and the body intrinsically fused. *Earth to earth, ashes to ashes, dust to dust*, goes a phrase from the funeral service in the *Book of Common Prayer* when the body is committed to the ground.

∽

But, if the land and the traces of the people here teach me one thing, it is this: religious and sacred are not the same, that is, when religious identity merges with national identity. Germany of the 1930s embraced an identity that conflated Christianity with the idea of a German *Volk* and Aryan race. As Mennonite historians say, religious traditions merged with a prevailing national ethos.[4]

4. Schroeder, "Mennonite-Nazi Collaboration," 6. Schroeder refers to work by Diether Goetz Lichdi and Mark A. Jantzen.

Some cultures hold that the earth, the land, is sacred, whereas within Christianity the idea in Genesis of subduing the earth was interpreted to mean a hierarchical cultural mandate that has been distorted. I wonder, as I view the river and fields, the crops and orchards, the wild poppies, the stork nests, the lindens planted long ago, an ancient oak, if the agrarian Mennonites here had learned to hold in tension the processes of subduing the land and being stewards of the land, also a scriptural command. *The earth is the Lord's and the fullness thereof . . .* But the parallel line that follows . . . *the world (is the Lord's) and all they that dwell therein* is particularly affecting in the context of Poland, the eventual ground of dispossession, displacement, and holocaust.

◠

The Polish people are restoring some of the centuries-old signature Mennonite house barns and estate homes, marking with signs these old farms of former Mennonite villages, as well as the churches bearing the official insignia of a heritage site. The cemeteries are identified with a plaque (*cementarz Mennonicki*), often announced with a sign on the highway, "tourist attraction" ahead. In places, the cemeteries, what is left of them, are being trimmed back with weed-whackers, in one village by the mayor's wife, in another by the Catholic parish that now owns the church.

Since 1945, the graves with German names have been disregarded, even destroyed. The Polish people, and more so the Russians, were intent on disremembering the former German inhabitants. But now the Polish people are caring for the remnants. They are interested in reconnecting with their shared history and the people with whom they shared the land before Poland was occupied by Nazi Germany, then governed by the Soviet Union; commemorating the Mennonites who, as our Polish guide Ewa says, "Took such good care of the land."

◠

Everywhere throughout the *Werder* there are imposing, red-brick castles built by the Teutonic Knights. Marienburg/Malbork is the site of the largest brick castle in the world, built by the order. My ancestors, and also my husband's ancestors, lived in this city, no doubt in sight of the Castle on the river. We both also have ancestral connections to Elbing/Elblag, where the oldest Mennonite church (1590) still stands, and I to the fortified cities of Danzig/Gdansk and Kulm/Chelmno. The history of the Crusades and German Protestantism is visibly juxtaposed with the later history of my Mennonite forebearers in Poland.

The knights of the Northern Crusades, the Teutonic Knights, rid the land of the Pagan Prussian tribes. Not much is known about these tribes because most of their mythology didn't survive, though scholars think their rituals and gods may have been similar to that of Lithuanians. What I can sort out is that under the governance of the Teutonic Order, cities such as Marienburg/Malbork were built as strongholds, in addition to the strongholds in the Hanseatic trade cities of Danzig/Gdansk, Elbing/Elblag, Thorn/Torun, and Kulm/Chelmno. The surrounding forests were cut down and the cities were populated with immigrants from Middle Germany, from where many of the knights originated.

There is a centuries-long history of power struggle and conflict between the Order and the Hanseatic traders, and with the monarchy of Poland and the heads of Prussia, but ultimately the Reformation impacted Roman Catholic Teutonic Prussia, as religious wars and upheavals took place (1519–1521). In 1525, an agreement was brokered between the King of Poland, Sigismund, by which his nephew, the last Grand Master of the Teutonic knights, would convert to Lutheranism and the land would become Protestant.[5]

~

Then, as in other places today, religion and geo-politics were inextricable. Between the lines of history is the open space of story. Where a culture has disappeared, or when there is a threat of its extinction, writers take up the pen. Nobel Laureates for Literature, Czeslaw Milosz and Günter Grass, are astounding examples in the twentieth century. Milosz, who became the voice of witness in the devastation of Europe, also wrote the novel *Issa Valley*, about life in a place that is both enchanted and haunted by its pagan past, and where the borders changed in war, when Milosz's Lithuania became part of Poland. The Polish-born Grass, in his novel *Dog Years,* employed elements of Prussian mythology to illustrate the reawakening of an ancient paganism and barbarism in Germany during the Nazi regime. Grass, who died in 2015, came to prominence in his writing about the crimes of the Nazi regime and German guilt, winning the Nobel Prize in

5. Wikipedia, *Teutonic Order.*

1999. Later, he disclosed in his autobiography, *Peeling the Onion* (2006), that in the last months of the war, at age seventeen, he had been drafted into the notorious *Waffen SS*. His critics would accuse him of hiding his own complicity until so late in life and even demand he be stripped of the Nobel Prize.

At the time my Mennonites were establishing their first churches, Crusaders were ridding the land of people steeped in paganism. Here too it must be noted that as Catholicism had become more rooted in Poland the Jews were regarded as "infidel in Christian eyes," and condemnation of their religion was morally authorized.[6] Four hundred years later, Nazi Germany flew the flag on which the swastika—an ancient religious sacred symbol from the east, a symbol also found in pre-Christian European cultures—announced its crusade against Jews.

And in my own family history, it would mean peeling the onion scales of our own stories, before, during, and after the war. By 1945, when Germany capitulated, all those deemed ethnic Germans were expelled from Poland and from all of Eastern Europe.

It was the largest population transfer in all of history—a chaotic and traumatic transfer of women, children, and old men by the allies, Britain, the United States, and Russia, that history has only begun to address. And the children who lived through it—our parents—now in their last decade and years, are cobbling together from old memories a legacy of both truth and transcendence for us who have no memory.

III.

One stone is dated 1723. The oldest graves—marked with natural stones, rounded, flat on the bottom and top—are deeply weathered, the carved inscriptions almost imperceptible. The more fervent genealogists in our group stoop over the stones with paper and pencils they have brought along for etching a name. Alan hands me a pencil but all I transfer onto the paper are fragmented marks. The Mennonite records of birth, baptism, marriage, and death were kept in the Catholic church here. A heritage site, this graveyard is in Tiegenhagen, in the *Werder*, just below Gdansk and this is the village of my paternal great-great-great-grandfather Heinrich, who allegedly left here for South Russia in 1803.

According to the church records, Heinrich was born *here* in 1781 and was married in the Tiegenhof church in 1799. His father Peter was born

6. Hoffman, *Shtetl*, 38.

in 1756 and died in 1796 in *this* village, although I find no stones bearing the family name. These forefathers are the descendants of brothers Jacob and Peter Letkemann, the first Letkemanns in Poland, thought to be of the original German Lutheran settlers who joined the Mennonites. Jacob died in 1757 in the nearby village of Altendorf. These two forenames, Jacob and Peter, have been passed down through history, to my paternal grandfather, Jacob, and my father, Peter.

Here, too, in Tiegenhagen, is one of the most fully restored Mennonite homes in the whole *Werder*. Designated a heritage site, it is made of large timbers and is in the process of being carefully reconstructed by a Polish craftsman, Marek Opitz, who is interested in the long-lost Mennonites of the region. Given that my ancestor Heinrich left for Russia, likely enticed by the promise of land, it is not likely he would have been as established as the original owner of this house with its land. In fact, a 1776 census indicates that his father, Peter, was not a landowner and was in a poor financial situation.[7] Nevertheless, this distinctively Mennonite house is still somewhat modest with its five square wooden posts in front; not round carved pillars as in other arcaded Mennonite estate homes we have seen, style and number of pillars being an indication of status. Opitz has painstakingly been returning the home to its original dignity, plank by plank by carved lintel, window frame and door, even preserving and replicating the original hues of paint, the interior pastel shades and bright doors and shutters.

And, it turns out, both my husband and I had ancestors who lived here. His family line, like my father's, would depart from Prussia for colonies in South Russia.

My father's ancestors would have left Tiegenhagen for the settlement in South Russia around the time this house was constructed. My mother's former home in her village is gone, though it would have been more a rustic timbered cottage in comparison to this house Opitz has labored over. The feeling I have walking through its interior space is hard to describe. The height of ceiling, the style of kitchen, a hearth, sunlight through a window spilling onto the wood floor become something innermost, as if a reclaimed memory from another time, another life.

~

7. Braun, *The Steppes are the Color of Sepia*, 8. Information is cited from an unpublished manuscript by historian Peter Letkemann.

Tiegenhagen is very near to Tiegenhof, the larger industrial center, where there were once factories and a distillery owned by established Mennonite families. In Tiegenhof, one woman in our group finds the house she lived in from birth until 1945. When her mother was ordered to leave with only a moment's notice she had been a two-year-old girl. She is now a septuagenarian with white hair cropped into a pixie-cut. Each of us on our own pilgrimage, her shrine a charming red-brick house with lace curtains in the window, on a street lined with brick houses. The only sign of presence is the barking of a dog inside but she is unable to enter her family's former home in the absence of its owners.

As we leave Tiegenhagen, I notice the small gauge railway that cuts through the fields and farmlands alongside the highway. The *klein bahn* tracks, which run from the main train station at Tiegenhof, past Tiegenhagen and other areas of settlement, was used by families to spend summer days at the Baltic seaside resort at the end of the line, about twenty miles away.

The ideal of homeplace contains only partial truth. In the return journey are the stories we seek and the ones we must also explore.

IV.

After only a few miles, our bus pulls into what looks like the driveway of an estate. Set among the large trees, almost concealed, is a stone manor house. Behind the house, a main gate, then sprawling fields. In the fields are the remnants of barracks. All is enclosed by a barbed-wire fence. A dense forest of birch stands beyond the fence. There, in the forest, the small gauge rail. Beginning in 1939, it was used to deport Polish prisoners, mainly non-Jewish, to Stutthof, where we now are.

Stutthof was a forced-labor camp, the first of such places outside of Germany, at first meant for those Poles or others living in Poland who resisted the Nazi presence, including up to 5,000 ethnic Germans caught in the underground resistance. The Stutthof camp system became an immense network of concentration camps for the Jews; 105 Stutthof sub-camps were established throughout northern and central Poland. Its major ones were at Thorn/Torun and Elbing/Elblag.[8]

It is late in the afternoon, around four o'clock, and besides our bus there are two cars in the parking lot. Our group is greeted by an older man

8. Wikipedia, *Stutthof Concentration Camp.*

in his eighties, slightly built, short, but standing erect in a plain black suit, white collared shirt, and black dress shoes. "For Poles, dressing formally is a sign of respect," Alan, our leader, will later point out. Stanislaw welcomes us, and states that our time together will be difficult but important.

By 1942, Jews from Warsaw and other areas began to arrive here. Some prisoners worked in SS-owned businesses such as the German Equipment Works (*DAW*), or in local brickyards, in private industrial enterprises, in agriculture, building dikes, or in the camp's own workshops. In 1944, a *Focke-Wulff* airplane factory was constructed at Stutthof.[9]

As we proceed through the gate, then through the series of bunk-houses constructed of plywood that impossibly slept up to five hundred people on narrow beds, three high, Stanislaw warns us that the following exhibit in the small wood shed will be difficult.

Mounds of children's shoes. "In 1943 there was a transport of children from Belorussia," he explains.

Gassing of victims began in June 1944 and continued through to November, done in trucks along these bucolic roads.

In a gentle, quiet voice, Stanislaw speaks in heavily accented but good English. We learn that Stanislaw is a survivor, that he spent two years in a camp, though not this one, until he was fourteen or fifteen, in 1945. I calculate he was born around 1931, the same year as my father, who is quietly listening, as we all are. That is all Stanislaw reveals about his own experience. I don't ask him questions about himself, or what camp it was. He is with us to talk about this particular place. As we walk along, he doesn't just speak of facts and numbers. In a clear voice, he reminds us of the importance of story so that we understand one another, of coming here to acknowledge what happened so that the next generation will not repeat the actions of a previous one.

The story of my heritage is tangled with this story, and is confronted by darkness; here, "the heart of a storm" as described by Milosz in his poem, "Generations." "Your destiny"—mine?— "is to run through the heart of storms," his poem seems to exhort me, "though all [I] wanted was to pluck a few roses."[10] As I recollect, I am re-collecting a previous life.

9. Ibid.
10. Milosz, *The Collected Poems*, 32.

I am learning that in the aftermath of violent histories, telling stories and listening to stories are acts of peace.

Walking through the camp, it has struck me how close it was to the villages, farms, and major centers we have been visiting.

As I walk through one of the wooden barracks I notice a document on the wall that lists names of those who worked in the camp. I pause to read them and one in particular catches my attention. A Mennonite surname flashes like an amber light.

In my later research, this name will be identified as a Block *Führer* and leader of a labor detachment. My subsequent enquiry will reveal the names of a few other men from Mennonite families who worked at Stutthof as guards. Did they think they might at least treat prisoners with a measure of dignity? How would they have answered if we could ask them why? Would they have said there was no other choice under such a regime?

Prisoners from Stutthof were deployed as labor on farms in the area, which, I will discover, included nearby Mennonite farms. Would these farmers have felt complicit, telling themselves that on their farms the prisoners would be treated better, at the very least, fed properly or at all?

Not only farms, but local Mennonite businesses and factories also benefited from leasing the slave labor supplied by Stutthof.

Later I will learn that as early as 1933, as many as 6,000 SS were stationed in the environs of Danzig (Gdansk), that this area was an early "stronghold in the Nazi revolution."[11]

I will learn that fifty-six Mennonite families lived in the village of Stutthof itself.[12]

And this: A Mennonite builder served as general contractor for construction of the buildings on the camp's premises.[13]

All this, our gentle guide must have known as he led us through, though he didn't speak of it.

Stanislaw led us, a group with Mennonite heritage from Canada and the United States, some of whom were born here and others whose parents and ancestors were, slowly through Stutthof. Stanislaw's own story was represented by this place, concomitant with our own stories.

11. Rempel, "Mennonites and the Holocaust," 512.

12. Ibid., 508, 517.

13. Ibid., 520.

~

At the war's end, all those in Poland and eastern lands with German ethnicity were imprisoned or expelled with the full support of the Western Allies.[14] The movement of German populations was considered unequaled in European history. Among us in our group are the droplets that had comprised a surging tide.

~

I am mindful that Stanislaw, my mother, father, and a few of the other older people in our group now in their mid-seventies and eighties, represent the last of the generation of living witnesses, children then. Our younger Polish guide, Ewa, a child born under the Communist government, also experienced the consequences of that time.

Showing respect to the other, listening to the other; surely there is something sacred in this.

~

Before we depart in the late afternoon, Stanislaw says something else that has stayed with me. "History shows us how terrible humans can be, only poetry can reveal how good humans can be." His words, spoken here, remind me of words spoken by George Steiner, the philosopher, professor of literature, and literary critic, born in 1929 to Jewish parents in Vienna. Steiner moved to France, and finally left for New York in 1940 to escape Nazism. As Stanislaw, in this place, indicates his belief in poetry, I suspect he must be familiar with Steiner who believed that implicit in the nature of the poetic is the notion of a moral imagination, grounded in love; a love that can transform us. And perhaps Stanislaw, like me, is a reader of Czeslaw Milosz, who believed that the purpose of poetry was to be a witness to disaster and to affirm life.

We speak the stories of those we love; those who have experienced what we have not; those who are gone.

To listen to a witness is to become a witness, Elie Wiesel had famously said.

14. Applebaum, *Iron Curtain*, 123–24.

He also said that for his generation, hope cannot be without sadness. But let the sadness contain hope.[15]

~

Walking through this somber site, this silent space bordered by forest, brings to my mind Rembrandt's painting, *The Good Samaritan,* which hangs in Poland's Czartoryski Museum in Krakow. The parable illuminates who one's neighbor is in response to Christ's question. How symbolic, the painting in dark tones, the large swirl of trees and distant forest, the circles of brown sky and cloud evoking the idea of a storm, and yet, a place of light emanating in the distance.

As I further consider the definition of pilgrimage as a journey to a place that has spiritual and moral significance, I realize that yes, Poland is such a place for me, too.

V.

The physical and emotional landscape of Poland, these places we visit, former Mennonite villages, the sites of holocaust, and the memories and juxtapositions they call up—disturbing, perplexing, poignant—bear moral significance.

As for spiritual significance, it's true many of the churches we have seen are no longer in use as churches. The Mennonite church in Elbing/Elblag, built in 1590, is the oldest standing Mennonite Church in Poland. The building bears a heritage insignia and is protected by law. In the bombing during the war, the church was the only building in the Old Town that remained standing. Its preservation is nothing more than a curious fact. Today the building is an art gallery. How appropriate, I think.

Other churches stand empty and abandoned, or are used for other purposes. A beautiful red-brick church in the *Werder,* the Tiensdorf Church built in 1865—though the congregation dates back to the 1500s—still stands. From the outside it looks as though it could host a congregation next Sunday, but inside it is gutted, and has recently served as a machine shed. Now the local men gather in the shade of the linden tree in front, sitting on old car seats, and drinking beer purchased from the *sklep* nearby. "*Dzien dobry,*" ("Good afternoon") I say, and the men raise their bottles as I walk past them to the church.

15. Wiesel, *From the Kingdom of Memory,* 202.

The church in Deutsch Kazun, near Warsaw, the first to serve the area where my mother's ancestors settled, and which could not be built to look like a church, is a wooden cottage where three families currently live; and in Wymyschle/Wymysle, my mother's village, the Mennonite church, rebuilt in 1865, is in disrepair, though it is a now a designated heritage site. There is talk about restoring it and using it as a clinic or community center.

The cemeteries too are in various states of repair. Some are beautifully cared for by Catholic parishes, or by the locals, after being much-neglected or destroyed during the Communist years when signs of Stalin's enemy, such as a graveyard bearing German names, were either demolished, or dismantled, the stones recycled for footpaths and foundations. At the cemetery in Stogi, remaining gravestones from other cemeteries have been brought to preserve their perpetuity.

And at yet another *cementarz Mennonicki*, among indecipherable and broken stones, there are signs of vibrant life, like blades of grass pushing through cracks of cement. Here, three young boys play soccer in the adjacent field, two tall grave markers moved here for goal posts; a tire hangs from the branch of the linden that was long ago planted at the corner of the rock foundations indicating where a church once stood. A man in our group has brought a bouquet of flowers. Sometime before he was born, before his family left for Canada in the 1920s, his grandfather was buried here. He looks but cannot not find the name. As this older man lays the bright spray of flowers at a stone with its name worn off, he knows, after traveling this far, it is the closest he will come to finding his grandfather's gravesite in this cemetery, among the fragments of a past life.

⁓

As for my mother's village, new houses are being built since we visited last almost a decade earlier. The village has become a bedroom community of Gabin, 11 kilometers away. A BMW drives down the now-paved road. There is even a sign *Infomacja turystyczna* (tourist information) in Wymysle stating in English, "One of the biggest settlements of the Mennonite Culture in Poland." The sign adds that "[i]t is still possible to see a stone church of the Mennonites from 1865, a ruined cemetery, and centuries-old cottages." But the pavement stops just before the still-empty site that was once my mother's former homeplace. Perhaps no one has claimed the property as their own. According to Polish law, those whose land was confiscated during the war may receive restitution if they are willing to give up their citizenship for Polish citizenship.

This village has been one of the best examples of a former Mennonite village that exists in Poland today, the way the farms are laid out and the number of original homes standing and inhabited. Even the deep well my mother's grandfather Kornelius Kliewer dug on his property is still in use, though the house is gone. On the other hand, the graveyard is more over-grown than in 2005. Like the church, the school is abandoned, the grounds filling with the growth of brush and trees. The kindergarten has also been abandoned since our last visit, its roof now caving in.

Here beside the former kindergarten, my mother encountered a Polish woman who had, in 1946, moved into a former Mennonite house which she still occupied, and had gone to the *skola* (school), the one a mile down the road next door to where my mother had once lived.

By this time, in 1946, my mother had been evicted from her home and banished from school, put to work instead. She would only have gone to the Kindergarten here, in 1944, her first and last year of school in Poland.

Two women with a divergent past and a village in common communicate—my mother's Polish limited but her comprehension still available to the other woman's language. The old gray-haired woman in well-worn polyester slacks, a faded, creased blouse, asks my stylish mother with her polished nails her age. Her face registers disbelief when my mother tells her, "seventy-five." "Same as me," she exclaims to my mother in Polish, her life in this village appearing so different from my mother's Canadian life.

This is where I have come from. Although I have not discovered gravestones of ancestors, or walked through, let alone seen, a family homesite as some in our group have, I discover a connection to place and to history, slight, tensile, resilient. I think of the massive web spun between boughs of cedar that I had seen on my walk at home in a Vancouver park. Alight with morning dew, its strands spanned what seemed a cosmic space. I had to stop and gaze at it.

$\sim$

The issue of identity is often raised in Mennonite circles, as one can be born a Mennonite, or one can become a Mennonite by joining the church. The question of how to describe what being Mennonite *is* came up frequently as we who were born Canadian were acculturating, individuating from family and community, and as some were leaving the church. What if one is no longer religious, or a member of the church? Is it an ethnic identity? At its core, this is sobering when I reflect on the past and the dangers of claiming an identity, national or ethnic, over one's place on the margins, the religious space where once the Mennonites resided.[16]

Mennonite identity is now referred to as a cultural, religious identity. However, there is undoubtedly a shared DNA stemming from the early practice of arranged marriage and the importance of retaining family land holdings. At a surface level, this genetic connection is a running source of humor among Mennonites. If two Mennonites encounter each other for the first time, they will always try to establish who they know in common. Often it takes only one or two attempts. And more often than not, they will discover they are related. Our group, starting out as strangers to one another, discovered that our genealogies led us back to the same villages, and that many of us who had never met before were distant cousins. As it turns out Alan, who convened our group and has led us through Poland, is my third cousin on my mother's side.

Even with a strong connection to people and place, I'm not sure coming here has deepened a religious connection to my Mennonite roots despite visiting the churches, but its traditions do pull at me gently. There certainly is a moment in Gdansk I will remember that seemed to bear significance—something that happens when people gather in commemoration and thanksgiving.

~

After a short bus ride beyond the old city gate, through city traffic, we arrive at the tree-filled hillside where the buttercream-colored house of worship stands facing the highway, on Mennonicki Street. Built in 1808 for the Gdansk congregation established in 1640, it became home to Mennonites who escaped persecution, and hundreds of years later was the site of the World Mennonite Conference in 1920. It's a weekday and quiet this morning as we file in through the tall doors, the date marked above them, and as I enter the building damaged severely in World War II, its exterior still scarred by shrapnel and bullet holes, I take in the silence, the light splashing onto the floor in the sanctuary, the wooden pulpit. I notice the

16. Huber, "Historians Address Nazi Influence on Mennonites at Mennonite World Conference Assembly." Scholars of Mennonite history state that the idea of Mennonite as an ethnic identity transitioned from religious identity after the war and grew through the 40s and 50s.

drum set, an indication of a congregation's generative thriving in this historical place with its worn pews. The high-backed benches creak like knees and spines as we take our seats. As I breathe in the scent of old hymnals and polished pews, I think of our Anabaptist ancestors who once gathered in this space, of what they believed in—separation of Church and State, peacemaking, service to others—and of all the ways in which these values were tested. We, diasporic Mennonites, sit together in the wooden pews with the morning light streaming in through stained glass, and then, spontaneously, lift our voices a cappella.

In four parts we sing the "Doxology" from memory, momentarily in harmony with the past, words of praise from 1674 filling the space as though more than just we are present here.

13

Sacraments

I.

Lent begins tomorrow. Ash Wednesday. The ritual of imposing ashes on the forehead, a sign of repentance and remorse for sin precedes the hope of Easter and the Resurrection. However, when I was growing up, it wasn't Ash Wednesday that marked the occasion of preparation for Easter in my Mennonite home. And in my heritage, the only fire and ashes that may have once long ago marked the occasion of Easter's arrival were those of the wood-fired ovens in Ukraine and Poland wherein women baked their bread.

As a young child, I knew that Easter was approaching by the sight of purple crocuses and golden daffodils thrusting up through the dark soil of my grandmother's flower bed. Moreover, Easter was imminent when the empty Roger's maple syrup, or Folgers coffee cans (the recipe in the 1962 *Mennonite Treasury of Recipes* states that "honey pails are also ideal") were lined up on grandmother's and mother's kitchen counters, greased and coated with flour to prevent sticking; the yeasty aroma of rising dough in the kitchen warmed by the pre-heated oven. Why the empty tins? Once the dough was prepared, "kneaded until smooth and elastic" Mennonite mothers placed it in the cans to give the *paska* its traditional and distinct round shape as it baked.

Paska, based on the Hebrew word for Passover, *Pesach*, has come to mean Easter Bread, a bread rich in eggs and milk and butter, eaten only at Easter time. *Paska* differs from Hot Cross Buns with their origins in Great Britain, popular throughout North America and available in bakeries and supermarket chains—also historically baked during Lent, but without dairy and eggs.[1] *Paska*, in the Orthodox tradition, is eaten after the Lenten fast is broken on Easter Sunday. Centuries ago, the Mennonites adopted this bread from their Russian and Ukrainian Orthodox neighbors, and while it is derived from the Orthodox celebration of Easter, it is a tradition so engrained in our psyche—or spirit, if you like—if you were to ask a child of Mennonites, he or she would think it was particular to *us*. In *The Mennonite Treasury of Recipes*, with its sections labeled "breads and rolls," "soups," "pickles," and "preserves," the recipe for it is in the special section of "Mennonite Dishes."

When our Mennonite ancestors lived in Eastern Europe and established colonies—moving from West Prussia to Ukraine—some Orthodox families lived among them in the settlements. The priest would come through the villages and bless the Ukrainian womens' bread. According to Norma Jost Voth in her book, *Mennonite Food and Folkways from South Russia*, in Ukrainian Orthodox tradition, *paska* baking would begin on Good Friday and was a serious undertaking, the Ukrainian women banding together to bake, their recipe consisting of a hundred eggs or so, mostly yolks, with corresponding pounds and pounds of flour and butter. The result was massive mounds of *paska*, risen and baked in the outdoor ovens, transported to the rustic onion-domed church by wooden cart. Though not to this extreme, the Mennonite tradition of baking *paska* would also be a serious undertaking but not one for which they took the blessing of a priest.[2]

Looking back to when I grew up, I'm sure my mother began baking before Good Friday, though—the yellow bag of Robin Hood flour, the Fleischmann's yeast, the butter and the fifteen or so eggs required. Even now, she prepares *paska* so it is ready for me before Easter so I can have some to serve my own family on Easter Sunday morning.

While I observe Easter, my tradition does not observe Lent, a time of repentance and fasting in preparation for Easter. Nevertheless, I gave up coffee for Lent one year, wine another year, chocolate another year, even

---

1. Wikipedia, *Hot Cross Buns*.
2. Voth, *Mennonite Foods and Folkways from South Russia*, 96–97.

bread once, but without much prayer or contemplation. "To feast we must first fast, to come to real consummation, we must first live in longing," writes the Roman Catholic Priest, Roland Rolheiser in the introduction to the Lenten devotional book I read to help me prepare.[3] I, the daughter of Mennonites from Poland and Ukraine who as children during World War II were dispossessed of home and country and family members and had experienced deep hunger and deprivation, can see why food and feasting, not fasting, had become a more defining aspect of my family's observance, or celebration, of Easter.

II.

Baking *paska* had its origins in pagan culture, adopted to the Christian tradition of Easter—one that replaced the pagan worship of the sun with the Christian worship of God's son. The history of the significance of bread to life, physical and spiritual, is as long as the history of agrarian cultures. Grain sheaves were an ancient symbol of resurrection as the wheat grows, dies, and grows again. Divinities in many cultures have been associated with grain, including from the Old Testament and the New Testament. I did not know those pagan stories as a child. But in Sunday school at my Mennonite church, I learned the stories in the Old Testament Scriptures; in chapter 16 of Exodus, of how God sent manna to the people of Israel. "Then the Lord said to Moses, I will rain down bread from heaven for you." Manna, white as snowflakes, or the cotton tufts we as pre-school children clustered on miniature chairs around the little tables used to glue to the image of a basket on construction paper. Manna, tasting like store-bought Wonderbread the deacons served the baptized adults at communion. In the New Testament, I learned that twice in the gospels, Jesus multiplied the loaves and fishes to feed the multitudes. A little boy's bread that his mother baked, my teacher said, his lunch, torn to fill basket after basket, the astonished disciples passing out the burgeoning bread to feed the famished crowd. In the Gospel of John, chapter 6, Jesus called himself the Bread of Life. "*I am*," using the name for G-d, he said—heterodoxy that would lead to his crucifixion—"*the Bread of Life*" promising those who believed that they would never hunger spiritually.

The Passover meal, the last supper Christ shared with his disciples in the Upper Room in Jerusalem was perhaps a simple meal. We know there was unleavened bread and wine, for at this meal Jesus, anticipating what

3. Pennoyer and Wolfe, eds., *God for Us*, xi.

was to come, told his followers to "do this in remembrance" of him as he broke the bread, and held out a cup of wine. In the aftermath of his crucifixion, the bread and wine became the sacramental rites of Communion, the Eucharist. Seated in the pew as cubes of Wonderbread and Welch's grape juice were passed along in silver trays by the ushers, as I experienced in the Mennonite Church of my youth, or walking in single file to the table at the front of the church to receive the elements from clergy in purple vestments, I continue to cherish the act of taking the bread into my mouth, whether by intinction, dipped in a chalice of wine, or followed by a swallow of juice from a thimble-like glass. In humility, and in community with others, I reflect, in silence, on the concept of grace. For a moment undistracted, I think about the fullness of love, unreserved, even lavish. The act of taking communion feels like a renewal to me; a metaphor for resurrection. Breaking bread, one Sunday a month throughout the year in my tradition, becomes a microcosm of Easter.

The theme of bread as ritual is one that runs through Jewish and Christian traditions. Commemorating the haste in which the Jews fled Egypt so that the bread did not have time to rise, the bread of the Jewish Passover meal is unleavened, while each Friday, *challah* rises and sweetens the kitchen with its aroma of yeast. Although *challah* does not usually contain dairy, it is perhaps comparable to *paska* in its golden color from the abundance of eggs, and in the idea of ritual bread. Friday before Sabbath, Jewish women prepare the yeast, deftly crack the eggs and apportion the flour for the dough braided and baked for their families. The name *challah*, derived from a Hebrew word, means "portion"—from the commandment in the book of Numbers to give a portion of one's gifts, whether dough, or an offering from the threshing floor, to the priests as was customary in those days. some baking *challah* today will still symbolically pinch off a piece of dough, as if a tithe, and burn it as though an offering, in commemoration of this commandment. *Challah*, first baked in the middle ages, was adopted by the Jews for the ritual Sabbath, then taken to Poland, Russia and Eastern Europe as the Jews migrated from central Europe.[4]

The origins and path of migration of these sweet and golden breads—*paska* and *challah*—with their symbolic significance to faith and heritage cause me to reflect on bread as the site of this convergence, and on the notions of bread as a symbol of a particular identity; bread as history and

4. Weinstein-MacCauley, "A Brief History of Challah," *Jewish website aish.com* (http.www.aish.com/?s=bc).

place made manifest; bread as both sustenance and sacrament. And bread, in all world religions and customs, as hospitality.

III.

This Easter, I have learned from my mother that my grandmother did not bake *paska* in Poland. Among the Poles, baking *babka* was the custom, a similar bread or cake but even richer with eggs, butter, milk, or cream: *Babka* is a version of the Polish word for grandmother. While she may have baked *babka*, my grandmother baked the bread at Easter traditional to the West Prussian Mennonites—*Streusel Kuchen*—simply made of a sweet bread dough from yeast, eggs, milk, butter, a bit of sugar, flour, and kneaded until perfect, risen, then rolled out flat, topped with crumbs made from butter, cream, flour, and sugar. My father's mother in Ukraine baked *paska* at Easter. But only "when we had enough white flour" comments my father who grew up experiencing Stalin's forced collectivization and famines. I imagine also, only when there was enough dairy, eggs, and sugar for the peasants after—if—the quotas were met.

In Canada, my Polish Mennonite grandmother's recipe for *paska* would have come from the *Mennonite Treasury of Recipes*. On the little ten-acre farm in the Sumas prairie, the eggs would have still been warm from the coop, from hens scrabbling for their food in the yard, the yolks the color of marigolds. Milk, frothy from the cow, a skim of cream, and the hand-churned butter the tint of sunlight, if sunlight were a color found in my childhood Crayola crayon box. The shade, taste, and texture of the bread unrivaled by the still-delicious *paska* baked today with store-bought ingredients. Baking *paska* would become a new tradition my grandmother from Poland gleaned from the women in her Canadian Mennonite church, situated at the end of the same country lane as their little farm, just as it had been in the village in Poland. My grandmother would have made some of her own adaptations to the recipe over the years, this rich bread yellow with egg yolks and churned butter and studded with raisins, or plain, that had been passed down one and two generations or more, then published in the *Mennonite Treasury of Recipes*. Recipes in Mennonite households vary from kitchen to kitchen as the baker and cook alters "to taste," and so each recipe, each loaf, or round of *paska* becomes distinctive of a particular household. By taste and texture I can tell the *paska* that comes from my mother's oven apart from the *paska* baked in another's kitchen.

And while Mennonites from Ukraine often topped their baked *paska* with a traditional cheese spread comprised of hard-boiled eggs blended with cottage cheese, butter, sugar, and infused with citrus from the lemon rind, my mother created her own cheese spread from Philadelphia cream cheese, icing sugar, and vanilla. My grandmother from Poland adorned her rounds of *paska* with a frosting of butter, cream, icing sugar, and rainbow sprinkles—the latter to the delight of her Canadian grandchildren.

When my grandmother died in 1999 at age ninety-six, we held her funeral in the Clearbrook Mennonite Church where she had been a member. Sacred hymns, a reading of the 23rd Psalm, and the eulogy recounting the story of her life, born in 1903, and set in the most violent time and place in that century, her journey through World War II, from the village in Poland to her final home, made up the service. Following that, in the church basement we held a traditional *faspa* of buns (*zwieback*) and cheese, with fruit danishes, from Funk's (the Mennonite Grocer's) in-store bakery, and coffee. During *frei williges*, open mic, when people say something about the person they are gathered to remember, a woman of about sixty came forward, a neighbor to my grandparents when they had lived on the farm on the Sumas Prairie forty years before. Her tribute was to say that my grandmother was a generous and helpful neighbor. And as if to give the ultimate example of those neighborly acts, she said, "When I was a new wife, Mrs. Schroeder gave me her recipe for *paska*. I still use it today. It's the best recipe." A valued gift of passing along a tradition.

I have let slip the tradition, the complex and ceremonial-like activity of baking *paska* in large batches, which requires methodical and well-practiced movements—first preparing the yeast in warm water, then separating the eggs, beating the whites to peaks and setting them aside, whisking the yolks with sugar until thick and lemon-colored, adding grated lemon rind, then stirring this into the milk and melted butter liquid. Next, gently folding in the whites and gradually adding some flour into the yeast mixture, which is now added to the whole, and at last, adding more flour, cup by cup, kneading, kneading until the dough is the perfect consistency—not sticky, and not too stiff. The glorious sight, the pillow of the risen dough, until double in bulk. Punching it down and portioning it out into the loaf pans that have replaced the rounded tins, to rise once more and take its shape before placing into the oven to fill the kitchen with the sweet aroma of fresh *paska*—the scent of Easter, as if incense. And here I am, letting it die.

Or will I? As I grow older, a longing, sweet and rich, for ritual and life's sacramental moments, rises within me.

Bibliography

Ackerman, Dianne. *The Zookeeper's Wife: A War Story*. New York: W.W. Norton, 2007.

Applebaum, Anne. *Gulag: A History*. New York: Anchor, 2004.

———. *Iron Curtain: The Crushing of Eastern Europe, 1944–1956*. Toronto: McClelland & Stewart, 2012.

Applebaum, Anne, and Danielle Crittendon. *From a Polish Country House Kitchen: 90 Recipes for the Ultimate Comfort Food*. San Francisco: Chronicle, 2012.

Braun, Connie. *The Steppes are the Color of Sepia: A Mennonite Memoir*. Vancouver: Ronsdale, 2008

Driscoll, Jeremy. "The Witness of Czeslaw Milosz." *First Things* (2004) 29.

Eksteins, Modris. *Walking Since Daybreak: A Story of Eastern Europe, World War II, and the Heart of our Century*. Toronto: Key Porter, 1999.

Epp, Marlene. "More than just Recipes: Mennonite Cookbooks in Mid-Twentieth Century North America." In *Edible Histories, Cultural Politics: Towards a Canadian Food History*, edited by Franca Iacovetta et al., 173–88. Toronto: University of Toronto Press, 2012.

Foth, Robert. "Geschichte der Mennoniten und MB Gemeinden zu Deutsch Wymyschle, Polen. Die Verfolgung der Deutschen in Polen (1938–39)." *Mennonitische Rundschau*, June—August, 1968.

Grass, Günther. *Peeling the Onion*. Translated by Michael Henry Heim. New York: Harcourt, 2007.

Guite, Malcolm. *The Word in the Wilderness: A Poem a Day for Lent and Easter*. Norwich, UK: Canterbury, 2014.

Hampl, Patricia. *If I Could Tell You Stories*. New York: W.W. Norton, 1999.

———. *A Romantic Education*. New York: W.W. Norton, 1999.

Hampl, Patricia and Elaine Tyler May, eds. *Tell Me True: Memoir, History, and a Writing Life*. St. Paul: Borealis, 2008.

Hoffman, Eva. *Shtetl: The Life and Death of a Small Town and the World of Polish Jews*. New York: PublicAffairs, 2007.

———. *After Such Knowledge*. London: Vintage House, 2005.

Huber, Tim. "Historians Address Nazi Influence on Mennonites at Mennonite World Conference Assembly." *Mennonite World Review* (24 July, 2015). http://mennoworld.org/2015/07/24/news/historians-address-nazi-influence-on-mennonites-at-mwc-assembly/.

Huberband, Rabbi Shimon. *Kiddush Hasem: Jewish Religious and Cultural Life in Poland During the Holocaust*. New York: Yeshiva University Press, 1987.

Bibliography

Kamieńska, Anna. *Astonishments*. Translated by Grażyna Drabik and David Curzon. Brewster, MA: Paraclete, 2007.

———. *In that Great River: A Notebook*. Translated by Clare Cavanagh. Poetry Foundation, 2010. http://www.poetryfoundation.org/poetrymagazine/articles/detail/69535.

Kearney, Richard. *States of Mind: Dialogues with Contemporary Thinkers*. New York: New York University Press, 1995.

L'Engle, Madeleine. *Circle of Quiet: The Crosswicks Journal, Book 1*. New York: HarperCollins, 1972.

Levi, Primo, with Leonardo De Benedetti, ed. Robert S.C. Gordon. *Auschwitz Report*. Translated by Judith Woolf. London: Verso, 2006.

Ligocka, Roma, with Iris Von Finckenstein. *The Girl in the Red Coat: A Memoir*. Translated by Margot Bettauer Dembo. New York: Bantam Dell, 2002.

Marchlewski, Wojciech, "Hollanders During World War II and Their Post-War Situation—Social, Political and Economic Issues: Mennonites in Mazovia, 1939–1948." Translated by John Friesen. *Catalogue of Monuments of Dutch Colonization in Poland*. Ministry of Culture and National Heritage. 15 pgs. http://www.holland.org.pl/art.php?kat=art&dzial=maz&id=13&lang=en

Michaels, Anne. *The Weight of Oranges/Miner's Pond*. Toronto: McClelland & Stewart, 1997.

Milosz, Czeslaw. *The Collected Poems, 1931–1987*. New York: Ecco, 1988.

———. *Facing the River*. Translated by the author and Robert Hass. Hopewell, NJ: Ecco, 1995.

———. *The History of Polish Literature*, New York: Macmillan, 1969.

———. *Native Realm: A Search for Self Definition*. New York: Farrar, Straus and Giroux, 2002.

———. *Selected Poems, 1931–2004*. New York: Ecco, 2006.

———. *The Witness of Poetry*, Cambridge: Harvard University Press, 1983

Nathan, Leonard, and Arthur Quinn. *The Poet's Work: An Introduction to Czeslaw Milosz*. Cambridge, MA: Harvard University Press, 1991.

Norris, Kathleen. *Amazing Grace: A Vocabulary of Faith*. New York: Riverhead, 1998.

Orr, Gregory. *The Poetry of Survival*. Athens: University of Georgia Press, 2002.

Pennoyer, Greg, and Gregory Wolfe, eds. *God with Us: Rediscovering the Meaning of Christmas*. Brewster, MA: Paraclete, 2014.

Peters, Victor, and Jack Thiessen. *Mennonitische Namen*. Marburg: N.G. Elwert Verglag, 1987.

Ponomarenko, Fran. "Yurij Luhovy on the Making of a Film about Bereza Kartuzka." http://www.ukrweekly.com/old/archive/2002/050220.shtml

Rempel, Gerhard. "Mennonites and the Holocaust: From Collaboration to Perpetuation." *Mennonite Quarterly Review* 84 (2010) 507–49.

Ricoeur, Paul. *Memory History Forgetting*. Translated by Kathleen Blamey and David Pellauer. Chicago: University of Chicago Press, 2004.

———. *Oneself as Another*. Translated by Kathleen Blamey. Chicago: University of Chicago Press, 1992.

Robinson, Marilynne. *Gilead*. New York: HarperPerennial, 2004.

———. *Housekeeping*. New York: Picador, 1980.

Roth, John D. "Historians Confront Hard Truths of Nazi Era." *Mennonite World Review* (5 Oct, 2015). http://mennoworld.org/2015/10/05/news/europeans-confront-hard-truths-of-nazi-era/

Bibliography

Sarton, May. *A House by the Sea*. New York: W.W. Norton, 1977.

————. *Journal of Solitude*. New York: W.W. Norton, 1992.

Schapansky, Henry. "The Early Letkemanns." *Mennonite Historian* 15 (1989) 2.

Schroeder, Steven. "Mennonite-Nazi Collaboration and Coming to Terms with the Past: European Mennonites and the MCC, 1945–1950." *Conrad Grebel Review*, 2 1/2 (2003) 6–16.

Schroeder Thiessen, Edna, and Angela Showalter. *A Life Displaced: A Mennonite Woman's Flight from War-torn Poland*. Kitchener, ON: Pandora, 2000.

Steinbach Committee: Mrs. Peter Rosenfeld, Mrs. D.D. Warkentin, and Mrs. Jac H. Peters. *Mennonite Treasury of Recipes*. Steinbach, MB: Derksen Printers, 1961.

Steiner, George. *Real Presences*. Chicago: University of Chicago Press, 1991.

Voth, Norma Jost. *Mennonite Food and Folkways from South Russia, Vol. I*. Intercourse, PA: Good Books, 1994.

Wein, Abraham, ed. "Pinkas Hakehillot Polin." *Encyclopedia of Jewish Communities in Poland, Vol. IV*. Translated by Leon Zamosc. Jerusalem: Yad Vashem, 1989.

Wiesel, Elie. *From the Kingdom of Memory*. New York: Schocken, 1990.

Zagajewski, Adam. "Words Against Death." *The New Republic* (2005) 24.